GIRLHOOD
UNFILTERED

Published by Knights Of

Knights Of Ltd, Registered Offices:
119 Marylebone Road, London, NW1 5PU
www.knightsof.media

First published 2022
001

Set in Charter Roman / 12 pt

Typeset & designed by Tia Ajala

Printed and bound in the UK

A CIP catalogue record for this book will be available from the British Library

ISBN: 9781913311179

The Forest Stewardship Council® (FSC®) is a global, not-for-profit organisation dedicated to the the promotion of responsible forest management
worldwide. FSC defines standards based on agreed principles for responsible
forest stewardship that are supported by environmental, social and economic
stakeholders. To learn more, visit www.fsc.org

2 4 6 8 10 9 7 5 3 1

GIRLHOOD
UNFILTERED

CONTENTS

Introducing Girlhood Unfiltered Ebinehita Iyere

HEALING Pages 26-51

If My Walls Could Talk... Jaala Shaw, 16

Forgiving, Not Forgetting Maákare Brown-Dyer, 15

My Pain to Power Taliah Douglas, 16

Tiger Scars Mikayla Chin-Nicholas, 16

Ode to My Left Arm Monteyah Edwards, 16

Not Your Loud Black Girl Faith Robinson-Cox, 15

Deeper Thoughts Shani Raphael, 17

EMPOWERMENT Pages 54-91

Black Girls VS the Education System Ivié Imafidon-Marcus, 16

Act I Scene V Rachael Leonce, 16

Black To An Extent Luam Dawit, 17

Black Girl Joy Elisha Amoako, 16

Freedom To Dance Deanna Atkinson-Lloyd, 15

Identity Crisis of a Misfit Shay Ashworth, 18

RESILIENCE Pages 94-133

11 Stops Shannon Goode, 16

Top Girl Aaliyah Bailey, 17

What I Hear on the Stereo Racheal Oni, 17

Simpler Times Blessing Peniel, 18

Music in My Ears Angel Ashanti Owusu, 17

Past, Present, Future Parris Safo, 16

The Start Disnee Laing-Smith, 23

Closing thoughts Ebinehita Iyere

Introducing Girlhood Unfiltered

For those of you that don't know me, I'm the founder of Milk Honey Bees, a charity that supports Black girls, and helps them to flourish. This isn't MY full story. You're about to read a book that reflects the wealth of Black Girl experience and the challenges they are facing. I've been through a lot and survived a lot – like these girls. But essentially one of the biggest transitions of my life has been to become the person I needed for others. I talk about my experience here to give context to the role I play in these girl's lives, and the role they play in mine. But some details and personal experiences have been omitted, to give space to the girls' voices.

One of my favourite books as a child was *Handa's Surprise* by Eileen Browne. Carrying tropical fruits, showcasing exotic animals, and exuding so much colour, reading this book always left me anticipating my own surprise; a world that was rich, vibrant and ready to favour what I brought to the table. My mum never failed to remind me how just like Handa some children used to walk for miles back home just to get to school. I too felt seen, as I sported my single plaits that sprung up just like Handa's if they weren't secured by my own tropical fruit, my colourful bobbles from the local hair shop.

See, just like Handa, I was a little Black girl with something special to share. But also, just like Handa the presents I brought to the table were often taken from me without permission, and instead of being well-received and favoured were misrepresented and misunderstood.

In this book I will share with you my girlhood and the experiences of many of our girls today. So, sit back, open your eyes, ears and hearts, and take in *Girlhood Unfiltered*.

****

Independence is something every little girl craves at some point in her life, but actually achieving this can come with its own unforeseen burdens.

Travelling to Australia at 7 years old with no-one but me, myself and Winnie the Pooh on my back, was my first experience of independence. Going to the other side of the world would be my first adventure. Super-excited, I remember being dropped at the airport by my mum and dad and escorted by one of the lovely air hostesses to get checked in and board the plane. Whilst aboard, I had my own private bell, which I took full advantage of to call for drinks, answers to my questions and anything else I could think of. I rang that bell so much, the crew eventually ended up turning it off - to my misfortune, as when I needed it most, needed them most, no-one came, resulting in me wetting myself like the baby I really was.

I was so embarrassed.

Looking back, this was my first recognisable encounter with adultification. Davis and Marsh (2020) define adultification as:

'...When notions of innocence and vulnerability are not afforded to certain children. This is determined by people and institutions who hold power over them. When adultification occurs outside of the home it is always founded within discrimination and bias.... Regardless of the context in which adultification takes place, the impact results in children's rights being either diminished or not upheld.'

Despite being a curious, demanding, and potentially annoying child, I was a *child,* nonetheless. I was alone and deserving of care and support no matter how frustrating it got. Whilst this may have been overlooked on the plane, it sure wasn't once I reached my destination. My extended family in Australia were everything and more. It really was my home away from home. Whether it was being put in pink, puffy dresses by my Aunty-in-Law, or running up and down with the boys, my cousins, I felt all parts of me were fuelled, fed and accepted.

Back at home in South London, life too was good, with friends and neighbours becoming like family and Mummy and Daddy being my best friends. So, when my parents split, I really was not ready. Not only did I not see it coming, but I was not quite sure how to process this new dynamic. As things changed at home, so were things changing for me as a growing girl. As I got taller and my body changed, so did the way people treated me. My cheekiness was viewed as mischief. My child self seen as a giant. My innocence; guilty until proven otherwise. This was yet another experience of adultification, in terms of the treatment I received from others. Due to our culture, it was seen as natural, so it's only with hindsight that I can recognise it.

Entering Year 5, I moved to a separate building, a different playground and experienced my first male teacher. Meeting a teacher like this opened a whole new dynamic for me to navigate. This teacher was everything I was not: white, male, adult and in a position of authority. Whilst I was used to being reassured from my previous female teachers with nurturing activities and the odd hug or kind word, I sensed a coldness, a disconnect and fuelled by the lack of relationship would play up in his presence. With constant reminders that secondary school was around the corner, that the teacher was right and knew best and my feelings going unchecked and unacknowledged, I began to lose my own sense of girlhood. I remember my chair often being kicked by a boy behind me. I'd tell my teacher, but despite society often deeming boys as stronger than girls, it would appear I was not afforded the same grace. It seemed that in any normal situation we would have been opposite sides of the coin, perpetrator and victim, offender and offended, boy and girl, in this situation we were grouped together based on our similarities; Black, big and typically disruptive and therefore not 'worthy' of any further attention or 'open' to any form of correction, despite the fact we were only 10 years old.

This concept of being a big Black girl did not end at school but was instead reinforced through expressions and remarks typically made in African and Caribbean households. Labels like 'biggy biggy' became my new name, whilst I silently grew more body conscious and grossed out by my changing body; a process that should have allowed me to embrace this next stage of my girlhood but instead felt like a literal weight I had to carry and could not change.

With changes still taking place at home and taking place with me, I tried to protect the version of me I liked often by twisting the truth. One evening after school I was at LatchKey, an after-school club for kids like me, whose parents may have still been at work after school. There had been an American Football Tournament at the weekend, which I had been looking forward to playing in and that I had been talking about for weeks, that I ended up missing because I had to look after my younger sister who was claiming to be "sick". Gutted and totally embarrassed, of course I told them I had played when asked. My team had won the tournament and for those moments I felt part of something good; I was on top of the world. But I was sent to rock bottom when my lie was exposed. I continued to defend my 'innocence', I couldn't come clean now, but the looks on people's faces let me know they already knew I was guilty. I was no longer a cute girl telling porkies, but a big girl telling lies. I saw an escape from what was really going on, but they only saw 'a liar', a trickster, a fraud and in a sense that's who I became.

These are two keys things that I believe are needed in girlhood. It is crucial to have a space to be a Black girl and when you have a place to be a Black girl, it is essential to thrive in it. Although, it is important to realise and accept that not everybody will understand you when you do so. That the one thing you have got is you. Especially when you are in a place and space where all you have been taught with the other girls is how to be against each other. So, do learn through your experiences to build your own confidence, to understand and navigate your growth. It is about being able to speak up about what you believe and not what you think everybody else is doing. That is why Black girlhood is a very unique experience and nobody's experience should be capped to one thing.

I began secondary school, where I was no longer 'the tall girl', 'the big girl', but now one of many tall or big girls. Everyone had an identity, a persona, a famo and I had to find mine. Having a famo or family at school meant you had olders, 'big siblings' if you like, and other friends that you were affiliated with and had your back at all times. Getting sent out of lesson and put into classes with the older girls put me in a prime position to become that 'little sister' and grow the notoriety I desired. At home, things were getting more and more tense with my actual family at loggerheads over my behaviour, so school provided me a place to feel free, to be seen and garner the attention I longed for.

Cussing teachers, getting into fights, using my height and build to my advantage, the school became my oyster. But secretly, this was just a shell, a facade I'd slipped into, to work with the narrative given to me to the best of my advantage. Deep down, I still enjoyed reading Smash Hits and PopGirl. Playing football and visiting the library to read about David Beckham. Begging mum for the latest copy of Young Voices and sticking the posters I got from it on my walls. I was a girl split between three worlds, what it meant to be British, what it meant to like sports and to play, and what it meant to be Black. But as much as these worlds intersected for me, my friends and environment didn't make me feel I could exist in all three.

Today, I support young girls to understand that being Black is not monolithic. You can exist however you are designed to, and not how you feel you must, to be accepted or fit in, but at the time this message was alien to me. As I exerted my Blackness for my friends, I also displayed behaviour that to the systems around me fit the 'angry Black woman' stereotype. Constantly in trouble and troubled in their eyes they referred me to a white psychologist. Whilst this may have worked for some girls, this didn't work for me. Again, there was a disconnect, a lack of understanding that kept me guarded up and reluctant to change.

However, I did have a learning mentor: I remember acting out one day and meeting Ms. Murray. Ms. Murray wasn't black. but she was the first person to ask me 'how I felt' rather than discussing my behaviour as a problem. It's like, for the first time ever, I had a moment to put my act on pause and actually ask myself 'how do I feel'? Struggling to even find the words, I asked her, 'Can I draw it?' She gave me a felt-tip and I told her I'd need more than that. She gave me the pack and I remember bunching red, orange, green, blue, brown, yellow and black in my hand and just going for it. Colour, confusion, a mix of good, bad, ups, downs: ultimately, a messy masterpiece is what I left on the page. That was how I felt. That was my life. Visiting Ms. Murray became a kind of safe space for me, but, out of sight, out of mind – soon I was back to my mischief.

By Year 9, things had hit the peak for my mum, who was now a single mother raising two children. I was staying out late, not coming home and in her eyes 'throwing my future down the drain'. She thought if she could send me to school in Nigeria, it would straighten me out and surely things would get better, I would be better.

And so, like *The Suitcase Kid*, moving from my mum's to my dad's on a Friday after school, I was now being moved to a whole new country, with a whole new school and a whole new way of life. Nigeria had its beauty, but it too was misrepresented by some of its people. This promise of perfection my mum expected was overthrown by the culture of survival, the hustle that meant 'money talks'. Rather than unravelling the layers that had bound me for so many years, the grip grew tighter as I learnt that to survive and go unbothered all I needed was the Great British Pound.

For the 17 months I was there, I grew further away from my father, the only person I felt could see the real me and instead became more accustomed to a path of destruction. Returning to the UK, he was the first person I wanted to speak to. I called him and we spoke like no time had passed. And like no time had passed, my behaviour remained rocky, along with this idea that I was still 'the problem'. I had even started a new school; probably one of the most notorious schools in Lambeth. Of course, I felt like I was at home at this school, but my behaviour was still spiralling.

At this point my mum felt she had exhausted her options of getting me on the straight and narrow and, as much as I loved her, we still couldn't see eye to eye. I resented her for sending me away. As my behaviour pushed me further away from the child that was full of joy, so did the relationship with my mum. My actions were putting her and my sister in jeopardy, with Mum having to miss work for meetings about me and facing court for my truancy from school. I was affecting her health, the stress of raising me and my sister and worrying every day about my behaviour was wearing her down.

The systems that were supposed to help us pushed us further apart, telling me one thing and my mum another. The only option my mum could see left was for me to leave the house. She didn't want me to go into care, but she felt that perhaps if I could have my own space and take on that independence for myself, maybe then I would grow up and she could also have a chance of me not being lost to the system. We were both being criminalised by a system that should have supported us, and so this felt like the only way to make the best of a bad situation.

At 15, I was moved to an 18+ hostel on the grounds that I had finished school, and therefore could stay there, as long as I was not in uniform as I had just been placed on early study leave.

This was my time.

My opportunity to stand on my own two feet, do things my way, be the hostess with the mostess I'd always dreamed of. Iced Gems, Party Rings and Space Raiders were first on the agenda. But, from eating the Pick'n'Mix at Woolworths and buying snacks with my pocket money, to having to budget for my own groceries, life got real quick and I wasn't quite equipped to deal with it.

But I was Empress Ebi and Jefferies Rd was my palace and not just for me, but for my people, my friends, my community. It became the space you could come for a hug, a cry, just to chill or even to survive.

Jefferies Rd was in Stockwell and was very close to home. It was just inevitable for me to be who I was there. I knew the area very well as it was a local area to me; that's where it all started. But I don't think it matters where it started, because if it hadn't been that road, it could have been anywhere. The same actions would have been enacted, and we would continue to do what we were doing before.

I took on the role of Brother's Keeper, a term that has been passed down through generations of Black women. It's a feeling embedded in you and led to me naturally tending to the needs of my bros whenever they needed me. Doing what was needed to allow them to survive and thrive in the way I had learnt to. Be it taking what I needed, dipping in and out of shops to put food on our table, or giving them the words to say to a girl they liked, going with them to the hospital, or sitting with them in the police station, I was an advocate before I even knew what the word meant. Society would have painted me a delinquent, a troubled teen, an accessory to whatever was going on in the streets, but I just wanted to be there for my people. In these guys showing me their vulnerability, I got to offer them strength, allowing me to feel seen and them to feel free.

Whilst Jefferies Rd was my first space, my palace, it also became my first prison. I experienced my first heartbreak, my first raid and a number of other firsts here, that leave it as a memory tangled between joy and pain.

Deemed a safety risk in Lambeth, I was moved back to Peckham. Back to my dad's area, my comfort zone and, in my mind, back on top. It was supposed to be another fresh start but instead just became an easier place for me to exercise my reign. I was known and, vice versa, it was a community well-known to me. It is where being my Brother's Keeper was engrained in me. My dad always used to say, "You've got Peckham in you through and through", because although I grew up in Lambeth I was born on Queens Rd, Peckham. It is where I started.

When I think of my Peckham home, I will always remember the door. At first, I was so excited to be moving to the area, but when I saw the door, my excitement was shot down fast. I was sceptical when I first walked in, fighting flies with every step, asking myself "what is this place?". Going from excited and curious to scared and unimpressed, I remember thinking "I've gone from bad to worse.

This could only be bad to worse". But I soon ignored my scepticism and started to feel impressed and excited, as I saw the double bed that I didn't have before and the little studio of mine. I smiled so happily. It was everything for me. As much as Jefferies Rd gave me my firsts, I had an experience of transition in Peckham in so many ways, especially my transition from girlhood into womanhood. During that transition, the most memorable thing that happened to me was meeting the people that I did.

I got kicked out of college for missing classes, associating with what they termed 'the wrong crowd', my grades dropping and ultimately not giving two hoots. I couldn't have cared less, but a conversation with my dad changed everything. "Go back to education or I will disown you" were the words that became alarm bells in my head. My dad, who had now moved to Manchester, was hearing about my antics on the streets of Peckham. He was receiving calls from his people, expressing disdain at who I had become. His words rang in my head, a wakeup call that I'd ignored from others for so many years. This was my dad and, as much as this life had become all I knew, I never wanted to be forgotten by him.

Life was changing thick and fast, I was moving from teen to adult, and what came next let me know for sure.

One morning as I went to grab my unicorn onesie, I noticed a leak in my wardrobe. Up until now, I hadn't really been aware of adult problems, but this let me know I had to do something about it. I called the Housing people, gave them my details, and let them know the situation. Whilst they could fix the leak, they revealed they had no log of me being at the property. The person who had worked on my case and moved me had left and not actually passed the casework on. For two years, I'd lived in this hostel, unaware someone was meant to monitor, support, and check in with me. There were notes that had been reported back to my mum saying I was fine and had been visited, yet contact had never been made. On going back to Jefferies Rd, I found heaps and heaps of letters in my name that had never made it to me. Giving the impression I was uninterested or refusing support when I'd actually moved from this place a long time ago. The system that was supposed to protect me had lost me and not even tried to find me.

I had no time to feel sorry for myself. I had a mission I needed to fulfil, so that I didn't lose the only person I truly had left. I learnt from those letters that I was now eligible for a bidding number to get my own place, out of hostels. I had a real chance at a fresh start, a new chapter.

I enrolled at Morley College, this time with a new outlook that I believe ultimately saved my life. Education gave me options and opened up the prospect of going to university. I secured a scholarship to university, moved into a two-bedroom flat, and was on my way to becoming Ebinehita, or so I thought. Though I was beginning to try and wanted to prove myself, there were still seeds of anger and pain that created a push and pull between who I was becoming and who I was known to be. To make matters worse, being placed in a two-bedroom flat meant I was liable for 'bedroom tax' as only I lived at the property.

In this same property, I learnt about sisterhood and relationships. Even though I have grown up thinking and feeling older than I was, this property confirmed to me that I was a grown-up earlier in my youth. With everything happening, I navigated a whole load of firsts and relationships, but in that same time, my godson was born. My godson and my best friend Renita pushed me to make it through college. Renita and I enjoyed life. We enjoyed it very, very well. Even though she's older than me by a year and a bit, looking back I can see we were enjoying ourselves, but there were elements of trauma beneath that. But looking after a teeny tiny baby, especially in a run-down two-bedroom flat, gave me a purpose again. I fulfilled that purpose and I still do. All I did was look after him and nurture his growth like he was my own. Our stories, though they differ, have similarities that have kept us true to who we are and always would be. Nobody controls where you start nor where you end.

I fell deeper into debt, and nearly lost my home as the council failed to believe that I was going to uni and would be able to pay once receiving Student Finance. The pressure of the situation, the need to make my parents proud, and rediscovering who I could be and was at my core, led me to feel overwhelmed and suicidal.

Getting into uni and things being resolved with the council helped me for a while, but there was still so much going on behind closed doors. Studying Criminology and Youth Studies, we had a module entitled 'Girls and Gangs'. As a result of my Dyslexia, I had the slides printed for me in advance and a chance to flick through and see what was coming up. And that's when I saw her. An acquaintance of mine that the lecturer had decided to make the subject of the discussion. My blood boiled and I erupted with all that was in me. Who did she think she was? She didn't know her. This girl was more than an example. This girl was real and suffering like so many of us and here she was being used to prove a point.

I instantly regretted my outburst, as whilst I didn't regret what I'd said, I was taken back to my days at school where my actions led to me being removed from the environment I was supposed to learn in. I apologised quickly, but the lecturer told me it was okay. I didn't understand. My actions meant I would be kicked out. Surely. But my lecturer, Dr Tara Young, let me know it was okay to disagree, okay to challenge and critique. Whilst my passion may have got the best of me, this did not make me a problem that needed to be moved.

I was learning something new, something different, and I liked it.

As my studies developed, I reached out to Whitney Iles, a youth practitioner that I hoped to attain some work experience with. Giving her the rundown of who I was and why I wanted to work with her, she told me she knew all about me. That the work she had done with young people had referenced me and my stories. Me? My stories? As I tried to figure out how anything to do with me could even be relevant, she told me that before any work could be done what I needed to do was 'play'. To connect with my girlhood and play.

Third Year of uni saw me go through my hardest chapter yet. I lost a friend, became depressed and struggled. I'd go to Namco to play games with Whitney. I wasn't sure anything had really changed for me as my world seemed to be falling apart but looking back the seed had been sown. In my learning to play, my healing process had begun.

As I put the finishing touches on my graduation look, I was met by loud banging at my front door. Bailiffs were here for Council Tax. Could I ever catch a break? I pleaded that there must have been a mistake. I was a student; I couldn't owe Council Tax. The system refused to believe me yet again and it was only on showing my tickets to graduation did they allow us to take it up with their superiors. It seemed that even in the good moments, the honest moments, I found myself fighting to prove my innocence and hoping it would be enough.

This narrative is one that I noticed was not just bad luck following me throughout life, but something that others in my community would experience too. I naturally found myself becoming that voice on the streets, that person that used their connections inside the system to make a difference on the outside. This role I had embraced through the community became full-time work. One day, I was supposed to work but I wasn't feeling too well so I ended up not going. That day, in that same area, a young man was killed. Whilst people tried to comfort me, saying maybe it was a good thing I hadn't gone out, I felt guilty. I felt that if I was just there, if I had stayed alert, maybe, just maybe, I could have done something to help him still be here today.

Time and time again, I was told of this young girl whose story was apparently like mine that I needed to speak to. I wasn't really interested in working with girls but was willing to meet. Meeting Disnee was like meeting myself in the mirror. After so many years of being misunderstood it was strange to find someone whose story was nearly identical to mine. In speaking with her, I began releasing without realising. I began healing the girl that I had just locked up inside and tried to move on from.

The first time I met Disnee, I offered to take her to get her hair done. I honestly thought I would never hear from her again, but I did. I genuinely didn't know what I was doing, I just know that when she needed me, I was there and, when she didn't want me there, I was still there. We ate Nando's together, cried, laughed and even at times argued. I didn't know I was recreating a structure for the future. I remember I gave her *Milk and Honey* by Rupi Kaur and one day later she was calling me to meet up. Not only had she finished the book, but she expressed to me how our meetups were changing how she viewed herself, allowing her to express how she felt and giving her food for thought for the future. Could I do this with other girls? Could we start a sisterhood? A girlhood for other girls like Disnee? Like Empress Ebi? Like you?

And so, a space where girls could meet, talk and be seen for who they were, was born. Milk Honey Bees. Whilst it was never specifically for Black girls, it did become a space where a high proportion of Black girls were referred. It seemed that the system took the view that they didn't know how to understand and 'fix' these girls, but that Milk Honey Bees had the answers. Whilst it is true that Milk Honey Bees provides a place of support and understanding, it is not a place for 'problem children' with magical solutions. Instead, it is a safe haven for girls to share who they are, where they're at and think about who they might want to be. Understanding that no two girls are the same, even if their stories may be similar, is vital.

Milk Honey Bees became a safe space for Black girls to be girls in 2018. It became embedded into my full-time job through the charity I had been working with that focused on young boys, Juvenis.

The space we've created is obviously reflected in the essays you're about to read. I honestly find it hard to read about myself, but it's a real honour to hear that I'm seen by this group of girls in a certain light. The feelings that are expressed within these essays are an exact mirror of how I see these girls and of what they've done for me.

For too long our systems have vilified Black girls treating them as women, calling them out for speaking and making judgements on them for just how they show up. The media alone demonstrates this issue with tropes and stereotypes pushed in film and media. Why was Scary Spice scary when everyone else got to be posh, sporty, sexy or baby? Why are Black women always fetishized or sideline characters in the movies?

Black girls are still girls and deserve to be heard, listened to, and talked to not *at*. Behaviour is a form of communication and is too often misdiagnosed as problematic rather than seen as layered and in need of concern and patience to uncover. Milk Honey Bees works to break these cycles and stereotypes of the problematic Black girl.

I shared elements of my story to highlight how my pain has turned to purpose and the opportunity each and every one of us has to create a change for our girls today. Now it's time to hear from the girls of today.

This book is in three sections: HER. HER stands for Healing, Empowerment & Resilience. These are the three components that come to together to bring you back to yourself and encourage you to put all parts of yourself first. It's an ethos to help Black girls and women remember that healing is not a linear process, and that it can be done individually and collectively, and that growth can be creative and liberating.

In Healing you will read work from Jaala, Maákare, Taliah, Mikayla, Monteyah, Faith, and Shani, covering their journeys of growth through painful times and challenging moments. Empowerment will introduce you to Ivié, Rachael, Luam, Elisha, Deanna and Shay, and will encourage you to find power and agency in their words. And the Resilience section brings Shannon, Aaliyah, Racheal, Ashanti, Parris and Disnee to the table, in which you'll see that vulnerability and resilience go hand in hand. All three of these concepts work together as a whole, and much like the essays within, can't be fully understood without each other.

This is Girlhood Unfiltered.

Ebinehita Iyere, founder of Milk Honey Bees

HEALING

IF MY WALLS COULD TALK...

Jaala Shaw, 16

If my bedroom walls could talk, they would open their mouths and blurt out all the negatives and the positives that make me, me. They would expose me for who I really am underneath my hard exterior; that I was forced to build due to other people's failures. If those ivory walls could talk, they would take you through how they celebrated me during my best and comforted me during my worst. If those four bedroom walls could talk, they would explain who I really am. They would talk you through the good, the bad and the extremely ugly things that I consist of. They would whisper in your ear the similarities and the differences that I share with you. Those walls that hold all my deepest secrets would allow you to see through me.

6:30am. I wake up, ready to leave the four walls that comfort me, in order to go to the ones that confine me. Every morning I do the same routine;

it's painfully embedded into my brain. There are 75 days until I never have to go to that school again and I swear they couldn't go any faster.

Growing up, I was never really uncomfortable with my race. I was always quite proud of my heritage, and that proudness only continued to grow with me. Us Black girls, as a whole, are full of creativity and have always found a way to express that in our style. We wear braids with beads, eyelashes, edges, and extra-long nails that have all been called "ghetto" in the past. That, however, never seemed to stop us from being unapologetically ourselves; another reason why I'm so proud to be Black. There are a variety of images of our style on various social media apps, most commonly of the 90's and the 00's era. The problem that this has begun to cause, however, is that Black Girls and women are usually never given the credit that they deserve, for the styles that they have created. Many people of different races, mainly celebrities, take the aesthetic that is associated with Black girls, and accept all the praise that comes with it. They accept all the glory and worshipping given by society, whilst we, as young Black girls, are left with all the negatives. I think that this eventually causes a problem for us Black girls, as it eventually makes us feel that nothing that we do is enough. But it is enough. We are enough.

Sometimes I wish I could forget the routine, and never have to look at the crumbling brick walls of my school again, but not yet. As I fill in my eyebrows to perfection, carefully place the bonding glue onto my eyelashes, overline my lips in brown liner, and smooth lipgloss over my mouth as if it were honey, I think about the wonderful Black women who inspire me to be myself regardless of the outdated European beauty standards, and I thank all of the Black women for inspiring me to continue to love and accept myself in a world where that doesn't always seem possible.

It's **8:20am,** and here I am walking along the same cracked pathway, on my way to the institution that forces me to suppress my creativity, in the desperate hope of being able to complete a secondary school education. My face, usually painted with a smile, is now a blank canvas.

School and I didn't always have such a toxic relationship; it was once comforting for me. I used to see it as a second home in a way. However, as I grew older, I began to realise more and more what home was, and what feeling safe was supposed to feel like. Then I realised that school was nothing close to that for me and that it probably never would be. School turned me, from the child who buzzed with excitement in every lesson, to the one who simply observed and was constantly on edge. Year Nine changed me for the worse. I was out of school for a year and began to lose trust in everyone... even in myself.

3:35 pm. School's over now, and I can finally return to where I feel the safest: home. Here, I get to be me in the rawest form without any judgement. I get to wear what I like and speak how I like, without the fear of stereotypical labels being thrown at me. I'm allowed to just be me. I'm back again in the confinement of my four walls, the only place on earth that I feel truly the safest. Here is my safe space. The space where I allow myself to cry, laugh, paint, and read. The space where I allow myself to heal, and develop each and every day, until I am able to look back at the old versions of me and smile at my progress.

Here I am again. In the embrace of my four walls, ready to peel off the protective layer which I wear to protect myself from the outside world. Within these four walls is where I prepare myself to be vulnerable. Yes, besides the common stereotype, Black girls and women are vulnerable. Here in my bedroom, I can cast out the irritation that courses through my veins like liquid fire and be myself. The girl that I was, before life began to get hard, before I had to become more dependent on myself. Here, I am the girl before the struggles of Year Nine, with the same aspirations, except now I am closer to achieving them. I am closer to letting go, and closer to understanding myself. Finally closer to the healing journey that I've been on for the past two and a half years. The truth is that healing takes time, and that each of our journeys will be different but it is worth it. It's worth it to finally remove the weight from off of your shoulders and rest.

1:56 am. Here in my bedroom walls, I am finally able to rest.

FORGIVING, NOT FORGETTING

Maákare Brown-Dyer, 15

There are always going to be ups and downs in friendships; some people would say friendships are built on trust. But, what if you built up all that trust with someone just to find out it was all one-sided, that you cared enough for them but they didn't care enough for you – how would that make you feel? Hurt? Betrayed?

Some friendships I've built have been good, others bad; most were a bit of both. But, in 2021, just before Halloween, my 'friends' showed their true colours. I don't remember how it made me feel. Tell a lie. I do remember it, too vividly: it hurt. To think that everything was slowly starting to look good in life, for them to betray me. I think they broke my cycle of forgiveness. I couldn't for a long time, but now I can forgive without resentment.

My relationship with forgiveness changed as soon

as I turned 15. I think I've matured and understand it better. If you were to ask me at the end of 2021 about my views on forgiveness, I would've told you it wasn't real, and that I certainly never forgave.

Forgiveness: a decision to let go of resentment and thoughts of revenge. But it's also being able to trust that after you forgive someone, they won't betray your trust and do something like that again, even if you never forget their past actions.

I find it funny how someone can go from your best friend, the person who understands you like no-one else, to a stranger. To a person who now acts like they never knew you at all. My past friendships, they ended faster than they began. I'm not going to sit here and bash the thought of friendships, because trust me I've had some good friends in my time. But maybe they weren't good enough to stick around – or for me to keep them around. I act like I don't notice lots of things, I acted like I didn't see the side-eye you gave your friend across the table as I started speaking. But I saw. I acted oblivious, so I could keep my heart safe. I think I loved the idea of friendships so much, especially because of how long it took me to find some. I always thought of myself as the caring friend, too caring perhaps. I would always notice, when you came-in to school with a frown, or when your eyes looked red and puffy from crying. I always checked up on you.

But for me that wasn't the case. I guess I gave you reason to think everything was fine? Because in your eyes Maákare was fine; she was laughing and smiling. But it was a lie. A façade I kept up. I think I kept it up so well I started to convince myself that I was alright. I started to believe that I wasn't really upset or angry at how my life has been.

Something I have out of school that I have been surrounded by all my life is martial arts (SKMA Hapkido) – it's a Korean martial art, and by my 16th I plan to be a red belt. At the moment I'm a blue stripe, I have four more gradings to go before I move to the adult class. I enjoy martial arts; I think there's a very skilled way of being able to get your anger out during kicks without injuring yourself or others. And the community is lovely as well, very diverse and welcoming. I think Hapkido saved me from death at the time of the incident with my not-friends in 2021. If my injury had been just under my eyebrow, I would've lost my eye.

Trust is very important when it comes to my martial arts, I think I like the controlled setting. Some people believe it's all about fighting your classmates and using your techniques on them so you're ready in the real world. But, as soon as you get into a fight in the real world your sense of direction is lost; you don't know how you should act or defend yourself, you feel lost, and your adrenaline distracts you.

But, in martial arts you need to have loads of trust and patience. You have to trust that the person who is trying out their techniques on you isn't going to hurt you. You have to trust that you won't hurt each other when sparring. In Hapkido our techniques are controlled, and we learn to control ourselves in the real world.

I think this helped me trust the girls at Milk Honey Bees, a lot quicker than I have before. After the third week, I got used to the environment and understood how to express my feelings in other ways instead of bottling it up. I think it was very hard to get to talk about my feelings because I don't do it often. I went from not wanting to be around girls at all to being put into an environment full of girls.

So, I'm finished, I feel like there's so much more I want to say, so many people I want to talk to or shout at, but maturing means moving on and growing up. I'm learning to say no to people. But I'm learning to trust them too. And sometimes you have to give up on people. I didn't lose a friend, I just realised I never had one to begin with. To me, my girlhood is me learning to grow and mature as a person. Me learning that friends can be temporary, and you should choose your friends wisely. Show me your friends and I'll show you who you are.

MY PAIN TO POWER

Taliah Douglas, 16

Before secondary school, I was a well-behaved student, never got in trouble, always on task, respectful, and "a pleasure to be around". Then everything went downhill. My attitude changed. I began to get distracted very easily. I slowly gave up on school. I had a lot of time out of class, and meetings every week.

Apparently, I don't know how to express my emotions. But have they ever asked me how I feel? Does anyone care? Even if I do tell them, what will change? Nothing.

I've been told that I'm rude. I think I'm just honest and people can't handle that. Me saying how I really feel gets me in trouble. It could be my facial expressions or my tone. Even my actions get me in trouble. Having fun, like play-fighting with my friends, gets me put in isolation. Even in isolation, I don't feel isolated, because I like time alone so it doesn't feel like a punishment. Imagine punishing me with something I enjoy, but not knowing I enjoy it because no one ever asks. School is more like jail. Isolation, uniform, rules. Why can't we wear what we want? It's like they're trying to stop me from being myself. Another thing I've been told is that I'm surrounded by bad influences. What people need to understand is that we're still young and we do things that we might regret later on. Most of my friends are Black, and we all get punished the same way for the same things. It makes me feel like I should just stop caring and listening to everyone and everything, and if I feel like this then imagine how many Black girls feel like this as well.

But no one will know how we feel. Why? Because no one asks.

The people that judge me the most are the people that say that they care. Main example: teachers. My teachers say they are here if I need to talk to someone. Lies. When I talk, they don't listen. I could sit here and give advice to Black girls, but adults wouldn't listen to us anyways, so I'm going to talk to you. You, adults. I don't listen to people who judge my behaviour. The reason being is, if you're not helping my behaviour, then I shouldn't listen to you. However, there are people that do listen to me. My friends, and especially my mum and Ebi. They might not always understand but they try their best. Being a part of Milk Honey Bees makes me feel safe and comfortable; being surrounded by Black girls who can relate to things I'm saying, and who feel comfortable to share what they're going through, is a nice feeling. Milk Honey Bees teaches us to be ourselves and stand out, to turn pain to power, to find your inner Black girl through healing. Healing isn't easy but it is necessary.

I always get asked how I would like Black girls behaviour to be viewed. I never know how to respond because I feel like we should be treated like everyone else. But we are not. So my advice to teachers, parents and society is to treat girls with respect. We are more than our behaviour.

TIGER SCARS

Mikayla Chin-Nicholas, 16

How I Feel:

emptiness

FRUSTRATED   uneasy

OVERWHELMED   confused

My Scars:

MIXED
EMOTIONS

painful

unheard
story

BOLD

mine

Black Girls:

UNHEARD

INVISIBLE

judged

forgotten

MISUNDERSTOOD

ODE TO MY LEFT ARM

Monteyah Edwards, 16

My left arm, the arm that carries my pain, the arm that harbours my feelings of sadness. The arm that in my anger I hurt the most.

My school judged me for being me and made me feel like my behaviour wasn't normal. I felt alienated. I also felt like they judged my behaviour, and they just gave up on me and they didn't try to help me. This made me get out of my comfort zone and not open up to anyone about anything. Which caused me to take out my anger on people that don't deserve it and it just made me feel like I was getting distant from everyone and becoming more isolated. It made me feel like nobody wanted me and they all hated me when really, I was just going through a lot.

In Year 9, a very brutal situation happened for me, and the school didn't support me emotionally and mentally, which caused me to act out. I felt not listened to and felt like I had no support through any of it from the school. I just felt like they punished me for rubbish because when other situations were more serious than mine, I would get excluded for having a lot of sanctions in a month. This made me feel like they were picking on me and they weren't trying to help me, they were just trying to push me through the door. I was just trying to get help, but I didn't want to show I needed help, I didn't want to be seen as weak, so I bottled it up hoping for someone to realise and help me.

I just felt like the pressure was getting worse and so was my mental health. They kept making me feel like the problem child, so in my head i was like they are only gonna punish me and I've been there, done that. They all saw it as me misbehaving, but never as a cry for help which made me feel even worse about myself. Because they always made me seem like I was the issue, I always thought I was the issue.

I felt like I was being put under pressure, then after I wanted to stop it had become a habit; whenever I felt any sort of emotion I didn't want to feel. I hurt myself because I feel like nobody is there for me, and because loss of friendship, relationship and arguments with family and family not being there for me.

Then I got a mentor, and it really helped me. I feel like when my friends are listening to me and talking to me and helping me through my problems it helps me. Feeling listened to really helped me get to where I am today.

NOT YOUR LOUD BLACK GIRL

Faith Robinson-Cox, 15

At first glance you would think I'm your average, loud, annoying, arrogant, Black girl, but if you take the time to look deeper, which barely anyone does, you would see I'm just a teenager. A hurt one. A confused one. Struggling to handle all my emotions.

Dealing with the loss of my grandma is probably the thing that impacted me and my behaviour the most. Because it didn't just impact my life then, it's still impacting me now. Partly because I feel that as I was so young, I never really dealt with it I just pushed it away. I mean I was still sad, but I don't think I actually acknowledged what happened and grieved properly. That was the first time I remember feeling a different type of sadness that I still can't explain. Around her birthday and the anniversary of when she passed, I'm always extremely fragile and unstable. Anything could make me explode/switch. But because not many people know that, again I'm just the angry Black girl with no control. When I'm too loud there's a problem. When I'm too quiet, something must be wrong. I feel like I can never just be me, without people judging me. So, I started just being loud, taking everything as a joke so I don't break down.

There was a period in my life when I was so sad which eventually turned into anger. It got to the point where I didn't know why. I don't know if that anger was due to my dad and his inconsistency, school, my family, or just everyday teen stress. All I know is that I was frustrated with the world. At 11 years old I should've been a kid having fun in school. Except I was not. I was the kid who was always in isolation or at another school. Even though that was sometimes because I was having too much fun. At 11 years old I should not have had all that anger inside of me. I was too worried about my mum and her struggles with my dad to tell her everything. She knew about the friend drama but not everything I was going through. To be honest I don't even think I knew. So I did fall into the stereotype of being that angry Black girl and I've fought so hard to get out of it, but it's hard. I see people from my old school and all they seem to remember is the girl who couldn't control herself. But I am much more than that. That's my fault though. I put out that image of me, so no one saw me vulnerable. Being vulnerable is still a struggle for me. Being hurt emotionally by my dad over and over again, I find it hard to let people in. I don't believe my dad has ever intended to hurt me, at least I hope he hasn't, but to be honest I feel I hurt myself most of the time. I kept on letting him back in, allowing myself to be put in the position of being hurt again, I've been stuck in this cycle with my dad for years. He was always half here, half there. The fact that he left didn't hurt me, but the fact he couldn't make up his mind if he wanted to stay or leave did.

The biggest obstacle I am having to overcome is learning to express myself beyond my angry Black girl self, and what people see. I still struggle with it quite a lot but I'm doing a lot better than I was. Instead of exploding and getting angry like I used to, I have learnt to not let many things bother me. Which is sometimes a negative thing. There's such a thing as being too nonchalant, which is a problem. I need to find the right balance between over-caring and not caring at all. I still sometimes don't feel like I'm being seen for me, which is frustrating, but those times when someone does actually see me for who I am, I get a sense of relief almost like I am doing something right.

Ever since I was little, I've always been the kid with way too much energy. Most places I go, whether that's a new school or an after-school club, I'm always asked "do you have ADHD?". This is the question I dread because I don't actually know. My primary school did try to test me, but my dad said no. I still don't understand why. Maybe it was because he couldn't bear to believe there was anything wrong with me, or it was seen as a weakness – which it isn't.

Having undiagnosed ADHD has been hard. It's the feeling of knowing you're different and everyone telling you you're different, but then not being able to say why because you aren't sure if you have it. Many of my friends can just say "yeah I have ADHD" and that's that, but when people ask me if I have it all I can say is I don't know. "What do you mean you don't know?" I genuinely just don't. I would like to be diagnosed. I feel like it would help me to just understand and have a reason for why I am like this. I also think it will help my friends to understand me because sometimes I think no one does. SZA and Simone Biles are just two of the Black women thriving with ADHD. I know I could thrive like them.

In the future I would like to be more confident within myself. Hopefully in the next year or so I should have my diagnosis. To my younger self and other young girls with ADHD. Don't change for anyone, be you. There is nothing wrong with you, your brain just works differently. Different is good. Don't try to be something you're not.

Deeper Thoughts

Shani Raphael, 17

I just wanted to be loved.

Honestly my whole life I have asked myself this question: why do I latch onto everyone who shows me love? Why am I constantly watching my family from afar? Maybe it's because of my behaviour. Can behaviour really affect your relationships with people? Aren't they just supposed to love you from afar? How do I stop feeling this disconnection?

It's crazy how actions really do affect everything. I just wanted to be loved, I just wanted to feel loved by my dad. Why is it that he could love my siblings and not me? I was his first daughter, but it seemed he picked someone to play that role who wasn't me. I realised that I had tried to find my father's love in boys. I had already seen and experienced so many things at such a young age, I realised I had so much life to live but I felt like my life had already been lived. I still had so many things to see and experience. I just wanted to not be afraid. I just wanted to be able to feel comfortable to open up.

Why can't I be happy and loved? Why am I always waiting for something bad to happen? Why am I just waiting for things to go bad again? Can I escape this cycle? Why can't I just break free?

My journey has been a storm that is only just calming. As I get older, I'm facing it and I'm doing it well. The message I want to give to all young mixed girls battling with these feelings, to those who have experienced detachment is: you can do it. You will be okay. Life will get better.

Romantic love is something I haven't fully healed from, but I learnt. My first love taught me relationship taught me don't let anyone hurt you more than once and always choose yourself. I fell in love at such a young age; we were always together, and he met my family. In that relationship I was so infatuated with him that I thought he would change. I think throughout the first part of my life, I was in denial that my dad was absent. I always thought it was better with him than my mum, when really it was my mum that was the best person to me. She was my mum and dad. I didn't realise until my recent therapy sessions that I've been looking for my dad's love in boys. Every relationship of mine has failed because they're not him. I've only loved one boy back in my life, and he reminded me of my dad. Every boy had an unhappy ending. Like my dad had an unhappy ending. Then I realised I need to stop looking. I need to stop looking for love. Love will find me. I've realised I need to stop blaming myself.

Friendship love is a real thing. So are the breakups. My first friendship breakup was in secondary school, and she was one of the best friends I've ever had. During the five years I endured in secondary school I was filled with anger. That friendship helped me to not be angry, until one day I snapped and took my anger out on her, which I deeply regret. That was my first friendship breakup and it hurt deeply when I had time to analyse and heal from things. In 2020 I developed a friendship that I think showed me the chameleon effect. We had so much similar trauma it was easy for us to connect, but what I realised is that our friendship wasn't genuine and that was a connection that wasn't meant to be. Sometimes you have to take yourself out of friendships if it isn't benefiting you mentally.

Now I've got a new friend that I met through my first relationship. Even though that first love damaged my trust, I gained an amazing friendship out of it. He is such an amazing person to me; he has helped me through a lot of my trauma and has continued to be by my side through everything. He was honest with me, and that helped me develop more trust for him because it proved that our friendship was genuine and honest. I did wonder if our relationship could be romantic, but I realised this was my first genuine relationship where I had felt like I'd made a friend for life and that was enough for me. He became a brother to me and that was something I was so grateful for. I owe him the world. People make it seem like men and women can't be friends without feelings, but we have broken that stereotype with our friendship. He has always done right by me, given me the best advice, and is always making sure I'm okay. He's one of the bestest friends I could ever ask for and I'm so grateful he is in my life.

Your best friendships as a woman can not only also be with men. Men and women can be friends without sticky entanglements. Me and my friend are proof of that. Now I'm starting to heal and I'm figuring myself out more and growing from the past heartbreaks I've been through I'm starting to love me. I'm putting myself first. I have to start putting myself before others because my happiness is bigger. I've learned that communication is something that's important in all relationships not just romantic ones. Communicating properly and addressing my thoughts, instead of burying them inside of me waiting for them to explode, actually helps. I'm growing as a person by accepting the past and embracing the future.

I've learnt that I can do it. I've learned that if you surround yourself with positive good things around you, life is amazing. I used to hate life. I used to not want to get up in the morning. I used to dream of not waking up. But through my newer friendships, I've learned that I shouldn't live in the past, I shouldn't worry, and I can be peaceful and happy. I learnt you can't let someone constantly do bad things to you and hold you back from your happiness. I've grown as a person, and I've realised putting yourself first is the most important thing ever. You have to think about your present and your future. I've found happiness in my current life, and I know how to maintain my happiness and keep it.

EMPOWERMENT

BLACK GIRLS VS THE UK EDUCATION SYSTEM

Ivié Imafidon-Marcus, 16

As a child in primary school, we used to play a game called 'Black shoe, Black shoe'. It consisted of everyone linking arms and someone would point down at the shoes, eliminating them one by one. In my eyes, the education system is quite similar. Its aim? To alter the way Black girls look, dress and behave, resulting in Black girls having to concave in order to fit its standards. Why are Black girls falling through the cracks?

The game went: 'Black shoe, Black shoe, Change Your Black Shoe.' The education system wants us to change our Black hair and our skin too. It wants to eliminate our culture and eliminate who we are, because, unfortunately for us, it does not aim for us to go far.

Schools tell Black girls to cover up and hide. In fact, 47% of Black female students in the year

2019, ranging from years 7-13, were told to cover up their bodies on the basis that their clothes were 'too revealing' and 'too unappealing'. They scream at us and punish us with claims that we over-sexualise our bodies, but what they fail to realise is that the body I was born with does not affect my education. I fully respect and love my body. So, do not tell us that we're 'hookers' or 'prostitutes' in your efforts to reconstitute the minds of male teachers who see no harm in flashing long, hard stares that cause alarm, that make us start thinking of how we should cover up our breasts, bums and thighs. It's not our fault they over-sexualise us, but, in their eyes, it BECOMES our fault that they over-sexualise.

We have teachers, Black and white alike, who feed into the stereotype that Black girls are loud and aggressive, that we are ignorant and not progressive. Why? Why is it that when we stand up for what is right and speak with power, it causes you discomfort? For we shall not cower.

Statistics state that Black students are already three and a half times more likely than their white counterparts to be placed in low ability sets, which helps to hold Black students back from achieving their full potential. It's as if they expect Black girls to not be achievers. Like they assume that Black girls are incapable. This becomes something that is an essential part of the battle that we learnt to give in to. We are praying and hoping that the beautiful Black children of today become the leaders of tomorrow, and that they bring about change and are influential within their communities.

Unfortunately, there are some out there without a voice, who have no choice but to give in to the powers that be. This is dedicated to them. I speak for those who are unable to speak for themselves because they're frightened. I speak for those who struggle in environments that aren't built in their favour, leading them to have to put in double the labour in order to just be seen. I speak for Black girls who aren't afforded the same leeway as their white counterparts, who are excluded twice as much as their white counterparts, who are trying so hard to perfect their art, and as a result, are downplayed from the start. I speak for that group of Black girls in the playground, all blissful, boisterous, and loud, who were told to split up as they are deemed gang-like and scary. What is the meaning? I speak for all Black girls who are receivers of adultification bias, forcing them to grow up before their time. A condition to the system that is perfectly sublime. Black girls are perceived to be less 'innocent' than their friends. A stereotype that will befriend them until the end. With the harsher punishments from higher powers slowly waiting to depower the minds of Black girls.

'The Georgetown Centre on Poverty's Initiative

on Gender, Justice and Opportunity' conducted research regarding the adultification of Black girls in schools in May 2018 and concluded that schools feel as if "Black girls need less nurturing, less support, less comforting and less protection than their white peers." Research consistently shows that Black girls are seen to be less innocent than their friends from the age of 5. We are grown women from birth. There is a lack of support for Black girls. Schools refuse to show up for Black girls. Why won't schools and society let Black girls be children?

I speak for all the broken hearts shattered by the darts thrown by those high up in power. They tell Black girls that they are dumb, unattractive, overweight, unworthy, and not talented enough. Belittling Black girls to the point where they believe this and begin to delve within themselves and seek insecurities. There is a lack of security, in fact, no security for Black girls.

School rules are not made in favour of Black girls. School rules are not made in the interest of Black girls. A white girl's mistake is met with sympathy and understanding but a Black girl's mistake is met with disdain and harsher handling. Black girls are two times more likely to be disciplined for minor violations, like hair colours or skirt lengths. They never highlight what Black girls do best. We are just discarded and looked down upon in comparison to the rest.

It's taken me five years to fully understand how to navigate the educational system as a Black female. I believe the realisation of my predicament in Year Seven hit me hard. I was big in all the wrong places, and girls' schools don't show any mercy, especially mine. When I joined, coloured hair was not allowed in my school, so wearing red box braids was a risky move, but they looked too good, so I was willing to rewrite the 'Guidelines for Girls' on scrap paper until my arm hurt and to be kept in isolation as if my hair colour would fade with time in the darkness of the room. I got tired of us all getting attacked for having subtle colours when the next 'Emily' and 'Hannah' were allowed to walk around school with hair that looked like neon highlighters, for goodness' sake. So, with the backing of Ebi, I brought forward the idea of the 'Halo Code' to my school. The resistance was immense at first. Our Diversity Lead was considerate of course, and sympathetic, but as she wasn't Black (and regardless of her hair being curly in its natural state), she'd never fully understand, she'd never fully get it. I had to go twice as hard for my people dem. I had to be thoroughly explicit and lay down the full facts. I had to give them no reason to deny me and what I was fighting for. It was sweet to see the change in the Guidelines on page seventy-two in our planners, I won't lie to you. I knew I had the power to change things and

I knew that this was the tip of the iceberg of what I could achieve. There is so much more out there waiting for me.

The clearest incident that hit very close to home was in Hackney. A strip search of a Black schoolgirl in the one place she was meant to be a child and be safe. Any one of my friends, my cousins, or my family could've been Child Q and that will always hit the hardest. *The Independent* described it as her being subject to "traumatic degradation", which is true to say the least, but what happened to her was cruel, ghastly, and most importantly **UNNECESSARY**. School is meant to be a place where we are allowed to grow, to be. But unfortunately, Child Q wasn't allowed to be herself. She is described now as a "shell of herself". We are continuously being left unprotected and are receivers of adultification bias, which negatively affects our mental health and body image. Two of the most important factors that are being taken for granted among us and about us.

I was desperate for an escape from my life at one point. Catholic girls' schools = wahala and that's a fact full stop. Juggling my autistic younger brother and the pressures of succeeding socially and academically at secondary school took a detrimental toll on my mental health, and I honestly didn't know what to do. And then that is when I found Ebi and Milk Honey Bees. The 6th of January

2021. I became fuelled with new knowledge from the BGGJI (Black Girl Global Justice Initiative) and was ready to open the doors that were previously closed by those who told me I couldn't do anything and that I was an 'overachiever'. They truly aren't ready for me yet. Suddenly, I had hope and I had something to look forward to.

Instead of conforming and being who they want me to be, I have decided to be who I want to be. I don't know who that is fully as of now, but I believe I should be allowed to at least have the chance to find out. I want the freedom to flourish and grow. I have decided that I shall no longer listen to the demeaning comments made with regards to how I look. I have decided I am no longer allowing stereotypes to define who I am. I am who I am because I am who I am. And that's a Nicki fact. Take it or leave it. I can throw endless facts and statistics at you, but that cannot force you to listen. I can pull out endless files of research and evidence formed to help those who aren't Black girls, in GENERAL, understand our perspective but I cannot force you to understand. It is only you who can choose to read and absorb. Only you can finally realise and go 'We need to start accepting Black girls, we need to give Black girls a chance'. I am a proud Black girl. I am bold. I am brave and I am comfortable in my skin. I am a Black girl without apology, and I am a Black girl without consent. It will always be Black girls vs the education system. It will always be Black girls vs society. The ideologies of society with regards to us will always be ingrained and hard to remove. It's time to try to defy. It's time, it's time.

What you choose to take from this essay, and all the essays included in this book, is beyond me, I know. But this whole book, filled with stories and anecdotes from a wide range of Black and mixed girls, wasn't just for fun. We didn't do it just because we could. We did it because we felt like we had to do something to finally make sense of everything we had been through. To clear the fog and express our pain. By voicing how we felt to release the trauma of our pasts, to allow our present and our futures to be greater. Being Black and being mixed girls and sharing our experiences could radically change attitudes about who we are as individuals. Our voice was needed to start the conversation we needed to have. The process of learning to speak up was so emotional for me that I stopped speaking for a long time. I stopped talking for a while, in order to protect myself and protect the people I cared about. I slowly found my voice, but not always as I had hoped, but that was alright. I am proud to know these girls because I know they are the type of women who won't settle for a life that is anything other than where they want it to be. A woman who is strong, intelligent, kind, compassionate and most importantly, happy. With a story to tell and a message to impart. The entire book, as I read and reread it, is rife with these themes and these real-life stories. To say that I felt like I had found a kindred spirit is an understatement. These girls, the women who wrote the book, gave me the support, the wisdom, the strength and most importantly the courage to stand up for what I believe in.

ACT I SCENE V

Rachael Leonce, 16

"Look like th'innocent flower, but be the serpent under't." — Lady Macbeth, Act 1 Scene 5, Macbeth

In acting, the first key concept you're introduced to is summed up in one magical word that sparks fires in little kids' hearts. Energy. Giving it your all, going above and beyond, redefining extra. Kids in theatre have reams of energy these days — it just spills out of them. Reams of fabric. Spools of thread.

At first glance, I can't really remember having that energy, at least not in a public space. I was that reserved kid who smiled at the teacher as she tried to settle a group of hyper seven-year-olds, or the one who always spoke too quietly when we were meant to put on a performance. "She's so quiet," the teachers used to say, "and well behaved."

That much was true... for public spaces. You see,

upon further reflection, I had my energy. There was a wild spirit in me, waiting for the moment to be released. Flashes of its dragon breath showed whenever my sister and I would hit play on the soundtrack from 'The Next Step' to then put on a showcase to our family (which really was just us throwing ourselves across the front room in an attempt at a modern contemporary dance). Scales of gold shone against my cheek whenever I hauled myself up two flights of stairs to stand and sing with my brother for a good two hours before we got the call for dinner. Brown eyes flecked with orange flames stared into the eyes of my beautiful mother when I sang 'Alone In the Universe' at my first performance I can remember, 'Seussical: the Musical Jr'. I had my energy; it was just redirected.

It comes with growing up. Finding friends, finding your space, aligning your energy. And I know all this 'energy' talk is starting to sound like I want you to join me on a seven-week mountain retreat where we do nothing but stare at the sun to align our chakras, but I think that people our age get scared as soon as the words 'finding' and 'yourself' are paired together. Rightfully so, too. It's so awkward —or wack as I like to say— this stage in our lives. I'm grown and *why do I have to iron everyone's clothes, Mum?* But then college application forms are thrust in front of me and I'm only fifteen and *Mum, I'm sorry about what I said last week but can you help me with this?* We can barely get out of bed at 7.30am for school, how on Earth are we meant to know who we are yet? Finding my energy, my essence, and focusing that on aspects I truly love is much easier.

But even that is a challenge in itself.

Naturalism. It's a term that's exhausted from its run in the acting world, yet very rarely makes it into the scripts. The art of acting as your character's most authentic self. Honesty and truth, yet a performance, nonetheless. Creating an illusion of reality. If expression of self is what I want to achieve, how have I expressed this?

Where does my naturalism start?

I'm twelve and my mum's just signed me up to this street jazz class. It sounds a bit different to the hip-hop class I'd asked for, but I guess I'll go see what it's about.

The first class is alright actually. The moves aren't too far apart from what I'd expected, and it's fun. Class ends, and the other girls start to take off their trainers to put on their ballet shoes.

Ballet. The word's enough to send shivers down your spine.

I ignore them and head straight to the car.

I'm twelve, so I don't think about it yet, and I'm scheduled to have the 'you're almost everything the world hates right now so you have to work ten times harder' speech in a few months' time, so life is good. Every Saturday I wake up at 10am to dance to the tune of serotonin, then catch glimpses of the other girls putting on pink tights and shoes that somehow match their skin tone. Rarely do I think about the pallor my skin would gain in those tights.

But I'm twelve, and I haven't gotten the 'talk' yet, so things are easy. I don't realise that the question of belonging starts here. I've never experienced the fear of being stereotypical yet — hell, I don't even know what that means! I'm twelve in the moment, and that's enough for me.

Next, I'm fourteen, and I attend two dance clubs now: my street jazz class which I'm slowly falling out of love with, and a more contemporary/lyrical class that I feel invisible in. I'm in the back row as usual, and nobody's spoken to me for the hour because, "Oh, I don't do contemporary. Sorry." But suddenly the teacher calls out my name and brings me to the front. He gets me to show the class how I execute one of the moves. They clap. "Rachael is actually really good," they say. "Well done!"

I'm fourteen, so I've had the talk. Remnants of it drift through my mind, but for the first time I got noticed in class. I feel my difference fade away, and I'm glad. I'm not ashamed to admit to only being well-versed in street style. They like me because I can move like them now. Life is good.

I'm fifteen and I've landed a role in a ballet musical. How? Only God knows. I still can't get a double pirouette, and my demi-pointe is horrific. I'm here though, so life is good.

Except, not really. Not anymore.

You see, I'm fifteen, so the talk is years behind me, but I've taken Media Studies for GCSE and that opens up wider perspective and retrospective thinking. Everything is stereotypes, diversity, representation — the whole lot. Every conversation must have a deeper meaning, and simply striving to be a Black actor who presents as a girl is a laugh in itself; the stakes are pitted high against me in this 'white, cis-male orientated industry'.

Yet, here I am, inserting myself in a none-too diverse ballet-orientated musical with little-to-no ballet experience and a vibrant love for street dance. I must be the laughing stock of the cast.

And I wonder: is this my naturalism? Is this my

warped illusion of reality? That I can adjust to such an environment as if I'm not different from the others? Has the fear of being a stereotypical Black kid conquered my otherwise steady soul, leading me to the stage with ballet tights that just about fit my skin tone?

I'm taken back a week to shopping for ballet clothing in a sports store. The rack glares at me, as I search for tights that resemble my skin tone and go over my feet. I need ballet tights, not jazz tights.

It hits me now. There are no ballet tights for people like me, people like us. On the shelf are pink, lighter pink, or nude jazz tights.

You may ask of the importance of the need for ballet uniforms to match the colour of our skin. In ballet, everything is about lines and extensions of the body, as well as the aesthetic. Ideally, there should be no disruption of the image of your leg as it stretches out behind you in an arabesque.

Pink is a very vivid contrast to brown.

It's hard enough when your leotard barely fits over your hips, but tights are a basic. I shouldn't have to stretch my nude jazz tights over my ankles to give the pretence that I'm openly welcomed into this art form, that it's accessible. Darker girls than I shouldn't have to 'pancake' parts of their uniforms to express their love for such a beautiful art.

I put on my shoes at home, and I feel euphoric. It's such a specific type of joy — validation. And yet, was the struggle to get these tights and shoes necessary? Do the others have the same issue? I finally fit in, but why do I feel so distant?

I'm fifteen, and I don't want to be different. I don't want to be the 'Black girl who only does street' stereotype. I direct my energy away from being the stereotype since fitting the stereotype is bad, right? I direct my energy to a struggle to feign diversity.

On opening night, the dragon in me sings. Curtains rise and I leap in my ballet shoes, I pirouette and land with my rising foot behind, I grin because I didn't turn the wrong way or fall. On closing night, I cry as I hug goodbye to the cast, I sob outside the stage door and block everyone trying to get past me, I open a Twitter account to thank everybody for the experience.

I'm fifteen and I sit down to think. I ask myself why I was called to the front when I was fourteen. I ask myself how I landed a role in that musical. I ask myself where the joy of what I do originated from. After months of questioning and false conclusions, I reach an answer: my difference.

That teacher called me to the front that day not because I moved like the others, but because I moved differently, because I'd never done contemporary before. I landed a role in that musical not because I performed like everyone else in that audition, but because I utilised my difference. It just so happens that my difference is part of a stereotype.

Realism. Portraying real life on stage. Who am I?

Being a Black girl who loves street dance is my realism. Being afraid to accept this aspect of myself and venturing into a vastly differing dance style is also my realism. Being in a ballet musical with a large street dance background as a minority is my realism. This is who I am. This is the content at my core. This is my realism. This is my naturalism. This is my *energy.*

Truthfully, this is only one scale from the dragon within me. I have a lot more to unpack, and I anticipate a lot of change as I do so. My energy is a ream of fabric I fold and sew into pieces of myself, yet never stops flowing. It simply spills out of me. Who would I be to bring shears to such a beautiful gold silk? The dragon in me is hungry; it's time to let it feast.

BLACK TO AN EXTENT

Luam Dawit, 17

Growing up, I've always known that I am of Eritrean origin. I mean, how could I not when both my parents refused to let me speak to them in anything but their home language and feed my stomach with injera (our traditional dish) every weekend, as a way of keeping our culture alive whilst living in the UK.

Eritrea is part of the Horn of Africa. East Africa. That's for those of you who are a bit rusty with your world geography. Most people may not know Eritrea, although now I guess Eritrea is slowly being put on the map, with all the Eritrean people growing famous. Deno, Rubi Rose, Nipsey Hussle, Tiffany Haddish. Those names ring a bell? Well, they're Eritrean.

What I love most about Eritrea must be Massawa, Eritrea's finest gem: the beach. It might not be able to top the beaches in the Bahamas, but I would say personally it's a close second. Oh, how I would do anything to be there right now. The sinking, thick, grippy, sensational feeling of your toes beneath the sand, the cool breeze engulfing you in its embrace, and the relieving feeling that all your troubles in life have diminished when you emerge yourself in the exceptionally blue sea water.

Whilst I've never struggled with the concept of where I am from, I more so struggled with my race. With being Black. Eritrean people are found to have a wide range of skin tones, with the majority having fair brown skin. All equally beautiful.

That's where I fit in. Brown-skinned Eritrean girl but, nevertheless, Black, right? You see, I never was Black enough to be Black. Not my own words, but from others. It was always, "oh Luam, you have really nice hair, are you sure you are fully Black? Indian maybe?". Or it was, "Luam you're not dark enough to be considered Black". Or "Luam you talk very posh, there's no way you could be Black fully?" So ironically enough, whilst many other Black women fought society to treat them equally in retaliation to the prejudice of skin colour and gender, I was fighting the same battle, as well as fighting people including my own brothers and sisters in colour in a battle to prove that I am Black.

Years of comments like these made me so uncomfortable in my own skin. I mean, what did you expect? A cut was formed, it got infected and, whenever a scab formed it got scratched and it got worse. In this case, I began to feel confused, insecure, and misplaced. The first comment made a dent in my introspection, and the more comments I got the more confused I became. Confused, because I began to question my race and identity, although I knew deep down that I was 100% Black. No questions. Insecure, because I began to cower away from conversations about race, because I found it too hard to explain to people that I was Eritrean, a place in East Africa (which I felt meant I spent a lot of the time arguing with people about Eritrea's geographical location) and that meant I was Black. I became afraid to have conversations like these with people, in fear of comments like "no way you're Black". Comments like that made me feel undeserving of being labelled as a Black girl. And I felt misplaced, because I didn't know where I belonged race-wise anymore, and if I could really call myself a Black girl. I thought I should maybe go by 'brown girl' instead, but wasn't sure I would fit there either, as it was a term used for South Asians – which I am not.

To add to this, every time I went to Eritrea, the place I called home, I was outcasted by the neighbourhood kids as well as my own cousins.

Even though I felt connected to my culture through the food, the semantic language of Tigrinya, and unique drum beats that are almost in every Eritrean music, there seemed to be a distanced separation between me and the teens of Eritrea. I am often described to have what is called an 'accent', which made it evident that I was not a local, creating an imaginary boundary between conversations initiated. In other words, I was 'whitewashed' in their eyes. I mean, I kind of was. I was born and raised in England, and it was evident that Tigrinya was my 2nd language not my first. This intensified the conflict that had mounted in my head for years about my identity and where I fitted. Where did I fit?

As I grew older, but perhaps not wiser, I found myself trying so hard to fulfill the stereotype of a Black woman, when actually I didn't need to fulfill this stereotype of Black women to create and form relationships with them. I didn't need to prove my Blackness to anyone, and I didn't need to act a certain way to be Black. In the last few years, I've grown in the sense that I've realised that there is no criteria for being Black that needs to be met. That criteria that I so needed to tick when I was younger was generated by white people to make us feel less than them. And unfortunately, this criteria has been used, by not only white people themselves but Black people too, to make some of us less included.

However, the good news is I'm quite immune to the comments now. Don't get me wrong, they can still get to me and I can lose all sense of composure in the climax of the absurd commentary, but I've learnt to smile and nod. Just by I'm smiling and nodding, I'm growing to love, accept and embrace myself more for who I am. In the words of Dave: "Eritrean, skin tone cinnamon, I think I found my princess". I am a princess, and my skin tone is cinnamon, and that makes me just as Black any other Black girl out there. I won't allow some uneducated human beings to take my Blackness away from me. My Blackness is one of the many things that make me, me.

BLACK GIRL JOY

Elisha Amoako, 16

What can I say? I'm a girl that likes to express her joy through many different ways. Especially through laughter. Some may think it is a coping mechanism, others may think I'm crazy but seriously I just like to laugh. It makes me happy. It makes me think of the good times and that not everything is bad. Laughter to me is like releasing all my stress thinking of positive thoughts and making memories, it means thinking of nothing negative and releasing all my bad thoughts. Laughter to me means to be stress-free, it means me being able to express my joy – it is me being able to release any bad thoughts because as I'm laughing. These thoughts are pushed away and no longer matter to me anymore. But when some people see me laughing, they think of it in a negative way, such as associating me with the "loud Black girl" stereotype. Why do I have to be associated with this? Can I not just laugh and have fun? But if you see a white girl laughing on the street, they would just think "oh she's having fun".

In my eyes, joy is the ability to think and feel and to be able to laugh and to spend time with my friends. When I think of Black joy, I feel confident and strong. Understanding my culture, that it was part of who I am, as well as being able to share my heritage with others. Black joy, to me, is also the experience of going to family gatherings and seeing my whole family together with smiles on their faces seeing that they feel free, happy in a space where they can truly be themselves.

When I think of the phrase 'Black girl joy', I associate it with many things. It means the family gatherings and the food that I'm able to cook, the smell of the food and being able to express my feelings with other Black girls and being able to relate, it is the smell of home, it is being able to celebrate with each other. Black excellence, seeing others thrive and being able to prove people wrong that the stereotypes are not the only things about us.

Walking in a hair store after a long day of fighting with my hair the day before and looking at all the possible choices of shampoos, extensions, and hair products you can use in your hair to make many different hairstyles that I get to choose for myself bring me joy. The smell of the hair store and the urge to buy everything in the store and me feeling that this store and home is the only place I can really go without being judged for how I look brings me comfort. I get joy from finding something that works properly on my hair and me not having to struggle.

Playing games after eating jollof rice and chicken and learning new dances to go with Afrobeats, laughing with my grandma and filming her for memories afterwards, is all what brings joy to me. Being able to visit my grandmother and bake with her for birthday parties, dancing to Afrobeats with my brothers, leaving African parties way after the time we were meant to leave, and hyping each other up is what Black joy is; it makes me happy. It is being able to express my culture around other Black people and being able to relate. But what does Black joy mean to you?

Black joy does not have one fixed definition even though when you look it up it says, "Black Joy is anything that inspires, supports, and uplifts Black culture." This doesn't mean that this is what Black joy is to you, Black joy can be anything you want it to be. Anything that makes you happy and what you enjoy, don't ever let anyone tell you that your definition of joy is not the right definition of joy. It could be you still playing with Barbie dolls, because who is someone else to tell you to grow up? At the end of the day there isn't an age restriction for it, it could be you cooking that you associate with Black joy, it could even be you expressing your talents, reading, writing, drawing, anything you want can be Black joy.

Personally, I did not feel I was able to fully express my joy until I hit Year 10, just after the first lockdown. During the first lockdown I looked deeply at myself and laughed at myself and said, "this really isn't who you are, and you can't be living your life as someone else." I can't be trying to be white when I am clearly not. Since Year 8, I've been the only Black girl in my year, so it makes it hard for me to really talk to my friends about my struggles as a Black girl as I know they won't understand and would not be able to relate. But as I proceeded through the years, I met more Black people through mutual friends and became friends with them. Many of these people were in the same situation as me. I was able to connect and talk to them about my struggles as a Black girl and we would overcome them together. We would also talk about family events and food and what we do that is similar, the things I was not able to communicate with the girls I go to school with. I felt safe in these Black spaces and felt happy, as it was never something I was able to experience before.

I never felt like myself before. I believe that I was hiding in someone that wasn't me, trying to fit in with everyone else just because the colour of my skin was not the same to theirs and my culture was the complete opposite. Acting like this whilst being the only Black girl in a predominantly white school made my outside-of-school friends question me: do you not feel left out? How do you feel happy or relate to people? They made me realise that I needed to fully express myself without feeling embarrassed or scared, because at the end of the day their opinion is nothing and should not affect me.

Black joy would burst out when I left the large wooden doors of my school and was able to see other Black individuals and communicate with each other just by one look. It made me feel like I was not alone.

When I was younger, there was nothing better than finding the only Black Barbie on the shelf, it was like a dream come true and I was able to play with it without noticing what was different and wondering why I looked nothing like a Barbie doll. I was fascinated by the only princess that looked like me and wanted to be her when I grew up. I also hoped one day to find a frog and kiss it to become my Prince Charming. Representation when I was younger and even representation right now is really important to me, it makes me feel as if I am heard and not overlooked. It makes me and thousands of other young Black girls feel as if they're appreciated and heard. Milk Honey Bees has done work with Barbie dolls, and when I was showed this work, I just said to myself "wow". What I really wanted as a child has become a reality. It showed me that anything was possible and that I should never give up. It was very important to me, as it was representation showing that people are able to make Barbies look like themselves. It gave me joy thinking about what else could become reality now that we have been heard as young Black girls.

The biggest lesson that I have learned about Black joy at this time in my life is that joy comes with pain; you may face painful days, but you will always get to the endpoint where you will be exceedingly happy, so never give up and never give in. Moreover, discover your own joy, someone else's joy might not be yours so do not be ashamed to show people what makes you comfortable and happy and makes you laugh.

Freedom To Dance

Deanna Atkinson-Lloyd, 15

What's the first thing you think of when you think of a Black girl dancing? Twerking (or doing dancehall and street) right? That's what you would automatically think.... Well, no that's not the only thing we can do as a collective: we can do tap, ballet, ball, street, hip-hop, Afrobeats, contemporary, jazz, break-dancing, the list can go on as we are multi-talented.

The way a Black girl moves is always a problem. If we aren't speaking or smiling people make an assumption that we are depressed or angry, or if we're in a group, let's say about 3-4 people, and in a shop 9 times out of 10 we are expected to get followed, when more time you have a top thief in the shop.

When I dance, I feel free, like a bee, as if a heavyweight has just been lifted off me. I just feel chirpy, it makes me express myself in a way I can't verbally. Me, personally, I dance like nobody's watching me, just like when you go to an audition and someone says, "sing like you're in the shower". The word 'dance' just reminds me of freedom, as there is never a wrong way to move your body. With dance, I express my feelings through different types of shapes.

When I dance the music, the beat, has a huge impact on me. For example, if I'm sad I will listen to something slow, or if I feel relaxed, I will listen to something slow but just a little bit more upbeat, and then if I'm in an energetic mood I will more than likely put on Afrobeats, because the tempo is upbeat, and it just makes me feel good. Through my years of dancing, I have learnt that as I move my body it tells a short story

The first time I remember dancing was when I was about two or three, it was a simple wiggle of the hips with a slight bend in the knees. It's all on video, me dancing with my brother at a party.

As a young Black girl, when I was in primary school, we used to play games like hop scotch, numbers (which is a hand-clapping game sort of like Ribena but much better) and making up random dances; inventing names for them which was really fun. Sometimes we used to do each other's hair, I mean when we were allowed because sometimes our hair just wasn't allowed to be touched (if you get it you get it), the rest of the time it was because our hair was in cornrows.

I've been to many different dance classes. I'm currently in one now and, I'm not going to lie, at first I did not really like it, as I didn't really know anybody apart from one or two people. I felt a little bit left out, because they were all in their friendship groups already, so it was just a bit awkward. They would all be in a group and me and my brother would just stand to the side as we didn't know anybody. As the weeks went on, I started to make lots of friends and socialise more, and I started to enjoy myself.

I used to hate... okay that's a strong word... *dislike* contemporary, because it just wasn't my thing. When I was younger, if I was to dance, like go to a dance class, it would be Afrobeats, ballet, hip-hop, or something along those lines. I remember the first time I tried contemporary, the first thing I said was "this is not for me" as it was just out of my comfort zone. Years went by and I finally tried it again, and I wasn't that bad – it was actually really fun. It made your body feel relaxed and light if that makes sense; it's just like floating on top of water. In my opinion, it's a spiritual way of dancing and gaining confidence plus creative thinking. This style of dance is usually done barefoot. I'm now 14 and I enjoy contemporary. It actually feels good to break the stereotypes with contemporary, because it shows we don't just do one style of dancing.

My biggest inspirations are my family and friends, and they are my biggest fans when it comes to me dancing, as they are always supporting me (like commenting underneath my dance videos, liking them, and reposting them). My favourite thing is that I'm not the only person that dances; my brother is my partner as well, so we make up dances together. It's like we are a just magical duo, we have been dancing with each other for the longest.

One thing that I couldn't forget to mention: Black girls not getting recognition on apps like Tik Tok. For example, Jalaiah Harmon; she made a dance called "renegade" which blew up world-wide and nobody knew that she made it, as a white person made it look like they invented it. But really and truly, it was a 14-year-old Black girl, so after some time she got her recognition which was good, but it still happens very often which is unacceptable.

When people don't get recognition, it makes me feel irritated, because someone else is taking credit for something they didn't even do. Then on top of that, people don't even make an effort to give credit to the creator, they just run with the fame knowing that it's not theirs. You should put DC: (then here you should put the dance creator @ or name).

Here's a little tip: when you dance you have to learn to let yourself feel your body movements to the narrative of the song. In other words, feel the music and the beat, not necessarily the words, so you can feel it more.

Identity Crisis of a Misfit

Shay Ashworth, 18

"How did you find the confidence to not conform?" Do you know how hard it is to answer that question? When the answer is just one big identity crisis, with me learning to get comfortable with being uncomfortable along the way.

Being born and raised in South West London, with 40% of the city being Black, I found a few things quite challenging. For example, being told that I must be Chinese, being asked "no, where are you really from?" when telling someone I was born in England, as if my combination is too complicated to qualify. The argument over whether I am brown-skinned or light-skinned, and the occasional "must be mixed". My favourite (not really) one was being told I look exotic (which in other words means I'm just pretty and Black, or a romanticised way of saying that I am foreign) by people that only wanna get close to melanin when it's golden. Basically, I was being called and labelled every name under the sun, and it really didn't matter what I had to say about it, the only thing that seemed to matter was how others perceived me. This was the beginning of me questioning myself: who am I? Who do I wanna be? And, more importantly, what should I be wearing?!

And so, I've never been comfortable in my own skin. I have always struggled with expressing myself. I tended to use art or continuous flows of bad behaviour, in school and at home, as an outlet of expression, but if I'm being real with you nothing compares to when I first started to explore myself visually. I remember the first time I stepped foot into the men's section of a clothing store. I was young, petite, brown-skinned, with hair bigger than my head either half-done or just out and free. It was winter; I was living with my Nan at the time, and being her favourite grandchild and all, I would utilise shopping trips with her. This specific trip I knew exactly what I wanted, I just needed to find a way to execute my plan perfectly. I spent the majority of my time walking around the women's section, until I found the confidence to go upstairs to the men's. On entering I got a lot of stares; boys staring at me asking if I was with another man or if I was lost and wanted assistance going back downstairs. Feeling embarrassed, and with my anxiety starting to rise, I began stroking the large-pocketed jeans, the baggy joggers, the hoodies twice as thick as the women's ones, whilst being filled with joy and want for these newly found garms. I still anxiously flicked through the boxers and the long socks and, if you're wondering, no, I did not buy a thing. However, that moment made me realise two things. One: the women's section is just not it. Two: I no longer wanted to be what society expected of me. I no longer cared what he or she deemed appropriate. I no longer needed someone to validate my thoughts. I wanted to be more, more than just the usual. I wanted to fall in love with myself, and not just hypothetically but genuinely. I no longer wanted to relate to society's views on femininity, my race, my gender. I figured I'd rather be an outcast then cast out later.

I remember the first time I wore clothes designed for men outside for the first time; it was back in 2019. After school, me and my closest friends at the time went to go pick up some girls from a school nearby. We hopped on the 432, sat on the top deck, at the back of the bus. I got changed there, and that in itself excited me as it was such an unwomanly thing to do. The looks I received, I was being judged, people were confused as to why such a lovely young girl was acting like mandem on the back of the bus. This was like a Superman moment – coming out of my disguise, revealing my truth, my comfortability, my freeness. Along with my hair, I wasn't very put together, my trousers hung low, and my top was two sizes too big, but you know what. for the first time in my life, I didn't look down to adjust my clothes and I didn't hate my arms or my legs. I wasn't too short or too tall. My chest may as well have been flat. I didn't have to lean against a wall to seem just that little bit bigger. I was comfortable within myself. It was definitely a step out of my comfort zone. Even though I was never the girliest girl, I always had my mannerisms about me. Unlike the way I'm dressed, you'd be surprised to know that one of my main focuses was hair. I like to think I'm quite good at it. I always do my friends' hair, and when people ask them who did their hair and they show me to them, their first reaction is always complete and utter astonishment. Like, no way I did that. Well, it's quite simple to be honest: I wear clothes made for men, not because I'm a man or wish to be one, but because I like them. The same goes for my hobbies; I do hair because I like doing it (plus I just happen to be really good at it).

Around a year into my new discovery, I felt like I had everything figured out. I was dressing how I wanted to dress, and I was a lot more confident and comfortable. That was, until I further discovered how not conforming to life had changed the way people perceived me. I was no longer that young, petite, brown-skinned, hair bigger than my head, either half done or somewhat just out and free, girl. I was no longer seen as innocent, I was seen as tougher than the other girls, I was now 'one of the guys'. Upon joining Milk Honey Bees, I learnt that it doesn't matter how I choose to dress, it doesn't define me, and that every Black girl has their own individual look. Having a space where I feel safe and can wear what I feel comfortable in became a really important thing to me. I can't imagine where I'd be if I didn't have this space. Even just the fact that, when we come into the Milk Honey Bees building, no one has to worry about fitting in. I can now proudly say I have a found peace in not conforming and by being myself. I believe everything I do makes me who I am, and I wouldn't change a thing.

RESILIENCE

11 Stops

Shannon Goode, 16

11 stops to get back to my roots and 31 minutes to feel comfortable again.

When I was 6, my mum told us we were moving houses; being young, I was excited about getting a new big room, and having my own space to play in as well as a bigger garden. Obviously, I couldn't really grasp the concept of moving areas and not being able to see all my old friends or seeing my dad every day – I was just really excited about moving houses and getting to design and have my own room. I remember being excited about getting my new school uniform, because it was a big change from wearing my own clothes every day to now wearing a shirt, tie, and skirt.

The first day of school was nerve-wracking because all my classmates had been together since the start of their school journey, and I had only just joined. I was one of two Black girls in my class, which was weird to me because I had just come

94

from a primary school with all ethnicities and races, where it wasn't common for the class to be predominantly white. I was young, I didn't really understand why this was. As I grew older, I noticed that I was living in a predominantly white area, and we were the only Black family on my road.

I remember only having one Black teacher in primary school. She taught us Music once a week, so it was nice to see I had something in common with at least one of the other people in the room. All my other teachers where white. I would notice that my other teachers would get really excited about how I wore my hair and, if my mum did it differently, they would all notice. Secondary school wasn't any different to my experience of primary school in Orpington, as it was still predominantly white, but I did notice a few more Black boys and girls, which made me feel a lot more comfortable knowing that there could possibly be a chance of having friends that I could relate to and not have to force conversation with, friends that I could be my natural self with. They would really understand me and my personality, and just get me on a level that my other friends might not get; I felt that I didn't have to over explain everything or re-educate them on what I meant.

Unfortunately, only two Black girls were in my form, and we were three Black girls in a group made up of again predominantly white girls. It was nice to have people to relate to, but I was now old enough to realise this is where I live now and we aren't moving again, I started to miss my old friends, and, although my dad did everything he could for me to be able to stay in contact with them, it's hard to keep up when you live so far away. I had to take a 47-minute train with 2 changes to see them as well as my dad, and then leave on Sunday night to get back home to Orpington to get to bed on time; I had to make sure I was able to have enough sleep to go to school early in the morning. It's long, I know.

From the ages of 13 to 15, my friendship group split up and I was the only Black girl left in my group. The only time I could feel like I wasn't the odd one out was when I was at Dance after school, down in London. I have a really close friend, whose mum runs the dance school. We met when I was 7, and since then she has been someone that I look up to in terms of dancing and acting, as she is an upcoming Black actress. She was the best big sister for me whilst growing up with 3 brothers, and allowed me to have a sister figure as well as inspiring me throughout dance school. To this day we are still very close, she helps her mum run the dance school that I used to go to every Monday and Friday. That was really the only time I felt like I fit in. I didn't have to question why it was so different when I was around my dad and back in London. But, then Covid happened and Dance on a Monday and Friday had to stop. We would run Zoom classes, but it wasn't the same. After Covid, I started to go to a new dance school with a friend I used to be close with at secondary school. It was weird, because I had again come from a dance school of all ethnicities and races and dance styles to a predominantly white dance school – and the dance styles were completely different, I tried out a few classes, but there are still not as many classes there as I would like to take. This was another moment that made me realise things in Orpington were different, and that I missed the normalcy I had come from. It made me miss my old house, my old school, and my old friends more. Things just weren't the same.

Then, I went with my dad to his office, and met Ebi. I didn't even realise I was a Milk Honey Bee girl until I noticed she kept introducing me as one. I remember that the first time I ever felt part of a comfortable Black sisterhood was at the screening of Rocks. To me, Milk Honey Bees is really important, especially because I felt a sisterly bond with Ebi, as I only have older brothers, and I knew that she would be someone for me to go to when I need advice or help. We did an online school called the Black Girl Global Justice Initiative with Miss Brie, and this is the first time I really got to learn about the things that other Black girls have experienced, and this helped me to realise that certain things that I may have not even noticed were adultification or discriminatory. By being a part of Milk Honey Bees, it has given me a space to gain more recognition of the things that happen to me in everyday life and be more in touch with allowing myself to feel emotions and not just push past them. I'm realising that it's okay to feel and be at peace with your emotions, rather than feeling wrong for embracing them. Also, I want to change things for younger Black girls, so the world realises and recognises that the young Black and mixed Black girls should not have to be treated the way we may have been treated; and they deserve to be heard and understood just as much as they are seen.

Stop one is Petts wood; that's when the music comes on and I mentally prepare myself for the amount of people that will avoid all the empty seats to come and sit opposite me.

When I get to Bickley, I relax a bit more, feeling the music playing in my headphones.

Bromley is where I feel like we may be getting somewhere with my very long and boring journey, even though I'm not even close to my destination.

Shortland's is the stop where I go through my

phone and try to find the most interesting game to play.

Beckenham Junction is where I really start to get comfortable with my feet up on the chair, and all my bags blocking anyone from sitting next to me.

Kent House is when I feel like I'm so close to getting off the train, but I've still got another 5 stops to go.

Penge East is where I feel the dull ache in my joints from being sat down for so long, the music doesn't help anymore and I'm genuinely bored.

The long tunnel between Penge East and Sydenham Hill is where I rest my eyes and think about what food I want to eat when I get to Brixton.

West Dulwich is where I continue to rest my eyes, but think what other things I can do to pass the short amount of time I have left.

Herne Hill is where I start to get excited, and I get out of my chair to finally get off at the next stop.

Finally, at Brixton I get off the train and feel content within my long journey.

TOP GIRL

Aaliyah Bailey, 17

You have probably heard the story of boys from Lambeth, well let me tell you a little about girls growing up in this borough. From before I was born, this postcode war has been live and in action: mothers burying their sons and teenagers throwing up more R.I.P's before they have left school than I can count on my fingers. A well-known issue of our time, this gang war spoken about but never enough or acted upon.

A lot of the time girls' experiences and trauma are pushed to the side, and the spotlight is on the boys when talking about youth violence. Like Ebinehita once said, behind every young boy is a bunch of mums, sisters, aunties, and friends trying to keep him off the streets, pushing him to stay on track. Whenever that young boy's house gets stormed by the police, there are mums screaming and begging to let him go. This is something that has been built so deep into our community and society: that women are just the armour that protect our boys. We are often told that it is men that have to be strong or handle it "like a man", but often women are put into situations that need to be dealt with maturely or professionally, without too much emotion.

Time and time again I have seen my friends and family get disrespected by the police, as I try to liaise or work with the police; my voice does not count for nothing. We have lots of provisions and help for boys who have been put through trauma in the community, but not enough for the girls who sat through trauma but didn't feel like it was theirs to claim as they were not the subject, even though they are still struggling with their mental health, still fighting the same mental battles as a boy. Yet, we are not taught to work through our trauma on youth violence or even know how to identify it. Sometimes it feels like it takes a girl to be exploited or violated in some way to get attention about their mental health. And even then, who's to say we are believed or trusted. Instead of being nurtured or cared for, we are judged, scorned for messing with the wrong boys or going down the wrong path. We are sick of being watched and penalised every moment of our lives; seen to act a certain way, talk a certain way, move correct and "ladylike". Short films, movies, news stories, I've seen them all and most never show a Black girl's perspective, unless they're playing the role of a honey trap or someone who ends up getting hurt.

We don't see us and I've always wondered why?

This year, when Season 2 of Top Boy finally came out, I was gassed to see Jaq, played by Jasmine Jobson, performing a role which turnt heads. Seeing a woman character hold so much status in a gang is not something we are used to. It isn't seen enough in the mainstream media: masculine women who still want to be seen as a woman. Some of the scenes were really powerful and said a lot without using words. (SPOILER ALERT) One that touched me was when Jaq was getting homophobic comments whilst out with her girlfriend and ended up getting beat up, and in the end found the boy who said it and got back at him and beat him up brutally and just wouldn't stop. That scene just really spoke a lot for me and probably the whole LGBTQ community as well. As in, yes we have had enough of this. Had enough of being told how to act our whole lives, from how to dress to what style to do our hair. Our whole lives being picked and pried at, to be made a product of our society. I feel like in the Black community as well, girls who dress more masculine are going to have it a lot harder than anyone else, because it's not just the world you're fighting, it could even be your own uncle, aunts, family who look down on you or talk about you and that is really hard. At the end of the day, girls never really get a say until it's too late and their whole life is already all planned out for them.

Trying to fit into an image that isn't yours is probably the best way I can explain my girlhood, yeah, I know quite sad if you ask me. Then another image could become projected on you subconsciously, which turns into your teenage years being controlled by social media and views, always looking for validation from anyone really, teachers or parents or boys. Then when we do get some confidence and learn some self-worth or find ourselves and our identity, we're seen as prestige or boujee or someone who forgot where they came from. It's crazy how much society can shape a young woman.

So this is how it went for me in Lambeth; the main profound base of my personality came from my childhood. I come from a family of 8. My whole life, all I knew was my brothers when it came to what I chose to wear, how I did my hair, how I spoke, honestly there was nothing girly about it. Despite my mother's efforts, trust and believe me when I tell you she tried her hardest to make me as "ladylike" as possible, it just never stuck. I'm pretty sure she gave up along the way. Growing up, I started to believe boys had it easy, they didn't have to cook as much as my sister, they were allowed to go out more and got away with more. I even got locs just because I hated having to take out my hair, it took me the whole weekend with my arms aching above my head, meanwhile my lil bro managed to take out his locked hairstyle in 10 minutes. Boys influenced my childhood a lot, but not in the way it influenced most girls.

I had some very interesting experiences throughout my school years. I went from loving who I was what I wore and everything about myself to thinking my clothes were weird and my locs were dirty, I ended up taking out my locs so I could get braids and feel a part of it all, the culture, the hype – to be honest I just wanted to fit in and it worked... for a while. Until a couple years later, when I was dressing how I wanted to and regretted taking out my locs; if I'm being completely honest I lost myself and it was hard. Feeling like I'm not who I was meant to be, feeling fake and false, is a real thing. Back then I never understood what was wrong, I was just depressed and didn't know what to do. I started losing my friendships one by one. Through all of these friendships going wrong, I was glad that I didn't feel false anymore. I made a promise to myself that if I wanted to make friends I would make sure I could be myself and didn't feel like a complete wannabe around them. In reality, I was scarred. I didn't want to make any new female friends, that was so scary to me, so I just rekindled the friendships I knew that I'd neglected and watered plants that wanted to grow. I learnt how to set boundaries for myself: 3 strikes, then you gotta go and I won't tell you why. This rule changed me.

With boundaries, comes more self-respect and by controlling who has access to me I was left with a handful of people who have my heart. I can be whoever I am around them without feeling a type of way and that's what makes me truly happy.

It's what I like to call a full circle; I came out of it all a confident young woman, who has great friends and healthy relationships around me. I have an amazing job with brilliant people, and also a place where I can be myself in Milk Honey Bees. I've met incredibly powerful, inspiring people in such a short time, I've accomplished so much in such a little time, and it really opens doors for young women at such a young age. I hope that you reading this take the time to remember who you are and be unapologetic for your identity, stay strong and walk through your community proud, never go unfiltered and always speak your truth.

WHAT I HEAR ON THE STEREO

Racheal Oni, 17

From what I can remember, I always used to fantasise about having the perfect girlhood when I was a little Black girl, from wishing my hair was like those girls on the relaxer box, to me being my true authentic self. Growing up with a learning disability was hard and having a lack of communication and speech skills was heavy for me. The fact that no one could understand what I was saying made me feel isolated from the entire world and closed off, placed into my own personal bubble which sometimes became quite lonely as the only one that could understand me was myself. Through this experience happening in my life, I felt like I didn't really have many people I could call 'friends', as my classmates made me feel like an outsider to everyone, I couldn't see anyone like this little Black girl out in the world.

As my little fragile self finally steps into the

milestone of life that is secondary school, I begin my 5-year journey of school feeling like I am on top of the world, making sure that no one messes with me because I'm that girl in town.... Well, that's what I thought in my head. At this stage of my life, people started to question me and who I was, but the big question that I started to ask myself was "who is Racheal Oni?". At secondary school, people had expectations of me as a POC (Person of Colour); for example, stereotypically POC, specifically Black girls, were seen as loud, 'ghetto' and having laid edges and long nails. as well as speaking slang, and when I didn't fit in to the stereotype people thought a Black girl should be, I was firmly labelled with words such as 'Oreo' or an 'inside-out Oreo'. The phrase 'Oreo' is used when someone is referred to as "Black on the outside, white on the inside" while an inside-out Oreo means the reverse. I would never have thought that comparing me to a certain food could define who I am. People put this 'label' on me as I didn't have many Black friends and because of the way I looked or presented myself.

This new insecurity of being 'not Black enough' made me feel embarrassed of my very own skin – something I'm meant to be proud of was turned into hatred, just because I didn't fit into a stereotypical box. Because of this, I was too scared to show my natural hair as people would stigmatize me as white just because I relaxed my hair, and I would try to change my voice/accent, as it was too high-pitched or people said I "over-pronounced" my words, and it sounded too "white". I would also try to change my clothes and wear skinny jeans and a cropped top with my braids tied up into a bun, because that's what you're 'meant to wear' as a Black girl. Through this, I was creating a fake character just for people's validation. I wanted the bullying and hatred just to stop but it never did. Each time I changed something about myself people said I was trying too hard and that nothing can change it; I was just white in a Black girl's body.

ONE DAY, I STOPPED TRYING TO FIT IN. Why does it matter? Why should I listen to the suffocating opinions of what I should act like, when it has only brought the worse out of me? **TO BE ME.** Why can't I just be me?

If I didn't discover this part of myself, I would have no clue who I am today. I looked to my Nigerian culture, and it made me, me. The first experience of entering the essence of Nigeria was a beauty to me, the heat hitting your face, feeling the bass of the song Kukere by Iyanya vibrating through your soul, to sipping that cold milo drink right after you had egusi and pounded yam. It was like I'd tasted the holy grail, and the energy of the happiest of Black souls made me feel accepted and appreciated. Nothing can ever describe this moment in my life; Nigerian culture made me feel the energy of being proud to be Black, to be me, to finally accept who Racheal Oni is. As I finally start to discover the nature of myself, I realize that certain characteristics, accents, even your clothing, does not determine how Black you are. Me being Racheal Oni, with the richness of melanin in my skin is enough, and the hatred and bullying made me have the courage to be just how I am as a Black girl.

Simpler Times

Blessing Peniel, 18

I miss those summers back. You see I live on an estate, which I personally think is the best estate ever, because you're basically in the middle of London and have a very lovely view over everything. There are three floors, and on each floor, there is a different group of kids and a pair of very annoying grannies. But even though we kids were all different, when the summer holidays came around, we all came together to play.

Man, I miss those simpler times. I remember my first summer with my first group of friends. The downstairs kids (the kids that live on the bottom floor): there was Casey, the cool lightskin and very funny kid, there was Laura, the white girl that always had the best snacks and looked after me like a big sister, and there was the new kid, the bad boy, Nicholas. There was one evening all four of us were chilling in front of the estate (it had scaffolding on because it was getting repainted). The sun was setting, turning the sky pink. And there we was, just talking. I honestly to this day do not remember the conversation, but it was one of the best moments in my life; no schoolwork, no expectations, no worries or stress, it was just us being kids, enjoying each other's company. In the real world, would this friendship group work? Of course not. But on our block, on our estate, it didn't matter.

A few doors away from my door lives a Jamaican girl called Rianne (pronounced rhi-ann). Although I went biking with her in the summer a few times, what I really remember is our winter breaks, back in 2011, when it would actually snow heavily in London. One evening me and Rianne played outside, we wrapped up heavily with winter warmers, mitts, scarves, everything. We played snowball fights and made creations out of snow; I remember an instance when I dropped a snowball on a moving car, the man in the car came upstairs and he wasn't quite happy and that ended the day after that. But even though that happened, I really enjoyed my evening with her.

On the block opposite me was my right-hand girl Rhinanna, she seemed shy but when you got to know her you always had the most fun with her. Always by my side, she was basically my ride or die, we'd do everything together (also we are both from the same country and our mums are best friends). I'd go over to her house to watch Bubble Guppies,

Peppa Pig, and more old cartoons. I had some of my best meals at her house, and she also had a big backyard so we would play outside with her cool toys. Sometimes, we would even have sleepovers at my house. She had a brother called William that would always run away, meaning we had to find him. She also had two older sisters, one very mean one (I don't think she liked me much), and another very fun and nice one.

There was also a boy that lived a few doors away from me on the same floor as well, his name was Antoine, he was like another younger brother of mine. One day I went to his house, where he and my brother were playing some type of game, and Antoine gave me one of his action figures: a pink Power ranger, He was such a neek, a nerd, a geek but that's what made him, him, and that's why I loved him as my own brother. There was also two Ghanaian girls that lived three blocks away from my block, Daniella and Latoya. Daniella was the loud dancer girl that literally had a crush on every single boy in the estate. She has two brothers, David and Denzel, who I found excruciatingly annoying. Then there was Latoya, the kind and rational one, that actually lived one hour away but would come and stay at her grandma's house in the estate during the summer holidays and breaks. They weren't part of the original kids, the ones I said before, but they fitted in like they were. And I had the best pre-teen moments with them.

One of my most favourite games that we played on the estate was football, on the grass cage. It was the ultimate rush, sometimes it would be boys vs girls, where Latoya would be the goal keeper, Danielle the defense, Rhinanna would be the midfielder, and I was the striker, but I preferred it better when it was mixed teams – it was way more fun that way. The only actual good players were me, my little brother Wisdom and Denzel. We would also play hide and seek, stuck-in-the-mud, and do our own mini-Sports Day. One time, in the middle of our Premier League match, Casey came and crashed the match with his mates. I started kicking at him and he started dodging; from then on, I realised that I had a crush on him. See the difference between him and Nicholas was that, even though Nicholas was extra good-looking, his personality was sometimes a bit sour, but Casey was funny, charming, and wouldn't try to act like a bad man; he was just him. So, that took him from a 6 to a 10.

Whenever we were hungry while playing outside, we would go out to our local corner shop and buy some sweets. I was never a sweet type of person: chocolate was my go-to. When two wings and chips was £1, we would always get that and eat together, but the best snacks never came from the shop; they came from our own houses. For some reason, snacks always tasted better when they were from someone else. I remember Daniella having a huge box, filled with chocolates, Galaxy bars, Maltesers, and M&M's. Danielle, knowing that I was a chocoholic, would only allow me one choice.

Birthdays with the estate kids were always the best. Carletta, the Afro-Latina girl that lives on the bottom floor, was celebrating her birthday with all the estate kids. At first, we were afraid to go in because of her massive Husky Luna, whose favourite thing was to jump on people, so Carletta's mum had to lock the dog in the balcony before we were able to come inside. We played some music, like Whip/Nae Nae by Silento, Gangnam Style, and birthday songs, and then we had cake and milk. There must have been something in the cake or milk, because me and my siblings vomited afterwards. I remember, for my 13th birthday me and Latoya went out to Clapham to venture around, though we didn't do much; just being with her was a birthday enough for me.

One thing that you could always expect around the estate was fights, and I would usually be involved in them; but it wasn't for the sake of it. I only got into fights when someone would pick on my friends, and I would usually only fight the pop-up kids (kids that only come during summer and don't actually live in the estate). For example, this boy called Jennelson was annoying me, and even threw juice on me. Some of the drink hit my little sister, so I grabbed Jennelson, swung him by his t-shirt, and it ripped. He went home with a half-ripped t-shirt, knowing that he should never mess with me again. There was also this really weird kid, that surprisingly had the same exact birthday as me. He always used to get on my nerves and, because I was flexible at the time, I would kick at him and chase him until I got the upper hand.

But the best thing, and my favourite thing about hanging out during school breaks with the estate kids, was the evenings, when even though it was 9pm the sun would still be in the sky. We would have silly conversations, adventures, like going to the parks around us and swimming in the lido, hanging out at BBQs and each other's houses.

Man, I miss those simpler times. But now everything has changed; none of the estate kids play outside anymore. Laura moved away, Nicholas got caught up in the bad boy lifestyle and I rarely see him, Casey hangs around the block sometimes but it's with his older friends and we don't say hi to each other, we walk past each other as if we have never known each other. I still speak to Danielle and Latoya sometimes, but we all have A-levels to focus on, so we don't see each other much. I see Rhinanna all the time, but she hangs out with her secondary school friends, and it's become awkward between the both of us. Antoine has gone completely off the charts, he's no longer the nerd boy that he used to be, but he's so caught up in trying to be this cool bad boy that he even gets into fights now. And it's not that times have changed, but society has; forcing us to become people we aren't. We were all bound to grow up, of course, to become teenagers and move on with our lives – but I will never forget those days, when the sun was never afraid to shine its hot beams on us and it didn't set till 10pm, when we were all kids, happy and free.

Oh, how I miss those simpler times.

Music in My Ears

Angel Ashanti Owusu, 17

I thought that life would be easy as I got older, now I can say that I was wrong. As a Black mixed girl, growing up in South London is very hard. I had people asking me what race I was, and I had people telling me that I didn't have my own race and that I couldn't pick whether I wanted to be Black or white. I've been let down by so many people. People have left my life; people have mistreated me and have taken advantage of me just because I'm a girl and that never sat well with me. It changed me, it changed my mindset and how I saw the world.

As a child, my song was Roar by Katy Perry, due to the fact that I always knew who I was and where I came from, and I'd always stand up for myself. My mum always used to say that I was confident and had the personality of a lion. This song spoke to me because it reminded me to never forget who I am as a mixed-race girl in South London, and that I would never let anyone take my shine away from me.

My other song was I Wanna Dance with Somebody by Whitney Huston. As you may already know, Ashanti loves to dance, it's who I am. Dancing is something I used to love doing with my dad. My dad passed away when I was ten years old. That broke me. Dancing with my dad was one of my favourite things ever. It was what we did, it was who we were. We were the dancers of the family, and any time we stepped into a party, people would beg us to dance because everyone loved watching us – especially my mum. She was our number 1 fan. I would do anything and everything to see my dad just one more time, and dance with him just one last time. Not a day goes by that I don't miss my dad; I was a little daddy's girl. I was his little mini-me, his little dancer, his little singer, his everything.

And the song that represents me now is Not Perfect – which is a song I wrote myself, because after all, I am a singer-songwriter. Not Perfect is a song that I wrote after losing my dad, being mistreated by boys, getting bullied, and acting a certain way to cover up my embarrassment and fears. I was so embarrassed; I felt like I was worthless. After experiencing all this, my mental health had gotten a lot worse. I started self-harming, because I didn't know any better and because I never spoke to anyone about anything. My song is not just a song for me. It's not a song that only I can relate to. It's a song that other girls around the world can listen to and relate to, just as much as myself. Song-writing helps me express my emotions and feelings. Because I'm not good at talking to people, I get scared of talking to people because I don't know what they might think about me. I write music to help me get on with my life in peace, and so that I'm not always so upset or angry or just continuously over-thinking things, and it's also my little get-away from reality.

When I slap in a pair of earphones, I just zone out and end up in another world from blasting music in my ears so I can't hear anything or anyone around me. When I'm feeling down, music is something that can make me snap back to my normal self and that changes everything in my day. I wake up, I listen to music. I'm in the shower, I listen to music. When I go out, there's music continuously in my ears. I'm always listening to music, whether I'm in a good mood or a bad mood. Music is truly my best friend and it's never let me down. Even younger Ashanti, you can agree you loved music, right? Dancing on the table in your little nappies to Michael Jackson for hours on end. Music is one of my biggest inspirations, and that's why I decided to become a singer-songwriter and artist. In the future, I'm going to live my dreams.

Speaking of the future, a song that inspires me for the future is Rise Up by Andra Day. *I'll rise up, high like the waves, I'll rise up, despite all the ache, and*

I'll do it a thousand times again. Those words mean a lot to me, because no matter what challenges I face in my life, I'm gonna keep going and I'm gonna keep chasing my dreams and not let anything stop me from shining bright like the star I truly know I am. My mum helped me realise that. She's the strongest woman I know. Even though I always used to think that she didn't know anything, I can now say that she really does. Most of the things I've gone through throughout my life, my mum has experienced the same things and she too has said it's not nice, it's not fair, and that those things will never sit well with her. After the things my mum has gone through, I can proudly say: that's my mum and she's my rock. I know that I didn't always show it, but I do love my mum with all my heart; she's the reason why I'm still alive today and I don't thank her enough. She's always there for me when I'm in trouble, when I'm down, whenever I need her, she's there no matter what.

So, to you, younger Ashanti: things aren't going to be easy for you in the future, but they will work themselves out for the better. You are gonna feel at times like you want to give up, but that's one thing you're not going to do, because you know you're better than that. You know deep down your mum will be there every step of the way, no matter what challenges you may face. Just remember what you're here for; remember what you want to do with your life. Prove it to everyone who doesn't believe in you. Make your plans, chase your dreams, get the help you need if you need it, and make your mum and dad proud. You are going to experience the worst bits of life, but keep your head up, because you're going to be just fine, and the best bits are coming.

Past, Present, Future

Parris Safo, 16

I question a lot of things about the meaning of existence, the meaning of the human existence. To be honest I believe I am the only real person and everything that consists around me is for the benefit of me and the life I live. Technically, you are not real to me. I do not share information like this often because it makes people think I'm self-centred or crazy but through the past three to four years I've taught myself that if they aren't real, then neither are their thoughts of me or opinions.

As soon as a person is born you are now in a system. A system that has been around for many years, meaning it wasn't created for girls like me (Black girls). Our differences and abilities weren't taken into account when this system was formed; we weren't a part of the system, our system was to work for free and to be tormented by society and now we must follow their system – that makes so much sense to me.

So, when I was born, I joined this system unwillingly and now it's finally a norm to me. I was born in England into a family of three; my mum, and two sisters who all originate from Jamaica. My father wasn't present at birth or childhood, which is just predictable according to stereotypes made by society. I just believe he chose not to be there. To be honest, he should never have come back into my life when he did, it was totally unnecessary. I lived with my mum for 16 years of my life, which wasn't a shock for me because my mum created her own system for her children. Her system stated that when her child turns 16, they must join the care system, as she can foresee the future and knows that the day you hit 16 is the day she will have problems with you. That was her mindset anyways. This system played out for all three of her children, including me of course.

My mum was born and raised in Kingston, Jamaica and had both my sisters there. When she came to England, she brought her daughters and her Jamaican mindset with her. Her favourite thing to do in the morning is rush her children to 'come out of mi hous' to go to school. It's like she purposely makes problems when you slowly approach 16. My mum also gave each of her children horrible nicknames she would call us when she was mad.

When I became 13, my mum had another daughter who is Irish and Jamaican (what a mix). She is my world honestly. She is currently 4, so she's got 12 years to go. I'm not a fortune teller or anything, but I believe she will break my mum's system. But. who am I to tell? Anyways, I believe my mum's biggest fear is embarrassment; she may not admit it, but I've seen how she is when she's embarrassed it's not cute for the person doing the embarrassing, honestly.

My dad was born in England, but his parents are originally from Ghana. That is it. No more characters wasted on that.

To be honest I can't complain, I had a great life until my sisters went through my mum's system and left. Then the process into Mum's system commenced for me. That's when it got hard for me, and I began to see how my sisters partially felt. My mum would constantly remind me I that would leave at 16, but I always laughed and told her I would be there forever. I really did think I would be there forever. But as I said I'm not a fortune teller so yeah. I went into care. Honestly, not really by choice. But it's all going well right now, so no regrets on my part.

Joining the care system was quite a rollercoaster. I say rollercoaster, because first I had to move from SE London to North London. And Monday to Friday, I had to take a train to and from school. If you don't call that a rollercoaster, then I don't know what is; I always felt sick at the end of the day. My carer was wonderful at the beginning. Gave a great impression to me and Ebi. Sidenote: Ebi was the one who woke up on a weekend (which is out of character if you know the Ebi I do) and booked an Uber from South London to North with me and my belongings. The Uber driver, Ebi and her bonnet, and me and my belongings, started my life in care for two years. Remaining time in care: 7 months.

I know I'm so unorganised, you should see my room. But I'm going to jump to how I met Ebi. Well, long story short when you have strict parents, you have rebellious children. I am the rebellious children. I would hide stuff in my school equipment, in this case it was a geometry set. That tin one. I brought my geo set to school, and the staff got me searched and I was particularly caught. My school gave me two options: a record or joining a scheme to help kids like me. F a record. Scheme it was. Ebi is the scheme. She introduced herself with Ian on a home visit. Ian explained his reason for coming and what he had planned for my Mum, as he was going to work with her as he stated. Then it was Ebi's turn. She introduced herself, and explained her plan with me and Milk Honey Bees. That's where my mum started to break her little act. Ebi mentioned working with young Black girls, like herself and myself. Dun Dun Duuuuuunnnnnn! My mum stated her mind and opinions on young Black girls and how they are troublemakers and 'legobeast', meaning they always on the road and loud and just aggressive. Ebi shut that down. Quick. I was shocked, I'll be real I was flabbergasted. Then, for the next 3 months I would have one-on-one counselling sessions, where I began opening up and coming out of the comfort zone I never even knew I had. I believe I'm quite a confident, well-spoken young woman (if you ask me). I used coloured pens which I hated – now I can bear them. I freed up Friday afternoons. I joined in with educational workshops like the Black Girl Global Justice initiative and interviews with Levi's.

I got to meet the girls Ebi spoke about working with. Now they family for real. We might not talk all the time or see each other, but we all know what it is. I confessed once in front of Kaia and Shay that I didn't know what self-care was. And it was true. They were all shocked, even Ebi. My next Friday session with Ebi, I was gifted a self-care package with face masks, candles, sweets, bath salts, bath bomb and snacks. I felt appreciated. I've never gotten a gift without an occasion, so it was a surprise. Working with Ebi has opened opportunities; I even got a first-aid certificate. I can approach and resolve a situation and put a person into recovery position.

That's a big deal at 16, if you ask me. Ebi doesn't know it, but she took me to my first concert.

When I think about my future: to be honest I want to be happy. I don't care where I'm at in life, as long as I'm happy with where I am at and happy with life. Not satisfied but happy. I believe that's the only real thing you can get out of life. Money is just a concept people agreed to follow, and that's why it works – if everyone stopped using money, it wouldn't be people's happiness anymore. I do want to go to uni, but will I, time will tell. I may do an apprenticeship, who knows. But I know I want to be a counsellor. Like I said, I'm not a fortune teller.

THE START

Disnee Laing-Smith, 23

Disnee was the first Milk Honey Bee, and her relationship with Ebinehita paved the way for the charity. In her own words, this is her story.

My name is Disnee-Terrene, I am a young Black woman raised in the heart of Deptford, South East London.

I began my educational journey at St Mary's Primary School in Lewisham, and then went onto St Matthew's Academy, also in Lewisham. I didn't have the most straight-forward childhood. I was raised by my Nan and her son (my uncle). My grandma gained full custody of me, and from then life began. Some would say I was spoilt, but I would say my Nan just loved me like her own. "A beautiful brown child; the curliest hair and the loudest cry" is how she would describe me. Growing up I was very boisterous, and by the time I was able to dress myself I was in nothing but tracksuits and trainers. I played football at school and table-tennis at after-school club – nothing girly ever amused me.

Fast forward to secondary school: I must admit I wasn't the most well-behaved. I was the typical loudmouth light-skinned girl, in the longest skirt that my Nan used to pay me £5 a day to wear. I was a big dreamer. In school, my biggest dream was to find my mum and all my siblings and live happily ever after. Sadly, my sister Chyna-Blu who suffered with cerebral palsy passed away February 10th 2014. It took a big chunk out of me, and I have never been the same since. After that I got excluded; I fought and my mouth used to run like a tap against any teacher, so much so that I found myself getting moved to Sedgehill School in Year 9.

Out of school, I spent a lot of time at Woodpecker Youth Club and hanging around the estates of Deptford. I made loads of friends out of school and would spend a lot of time in the Youth Club. Before I knew it, these friends had become family. We would all rush to meet up after school and get to Woodpecker. Woodpecker was home. The staff made sure we all respected one another, and it was like one huge family. Time went on, and the family grew, so big that we were now a gang: a gang full of talented footballers, rappers, artists. You name it, we had someone that could do it. At the time, without realising it, we let our environment get ahead of us. As a collective, we started to move into the street life and spend more time out of the Youth Club and more in the stairways of flats and on the 'block' – absolutely unaware of where this would lead us. Time went on and we had made enemies; we were officially a gang (a loyal one, I must say).

I became more and more boisterous, there was no lady left in me, and my priorities were scrambled all over the place. My grades were never ever low since primary school, they were always average and above if I wasn't misbehaving, but by now my behaviour wasn't the problem. My friend Myron Yarde (Mdot) died due to gang violence in April 2016. Another brother, Leoandro Osemeke (Showkey), died to gang violence August 2016. The two main characters of the 'gang' were gone.

I was 16 years old and absolutely lost. Cold-hearted, confused, suicidal. I just didn't understand how two best friends could die months apart. Was I next? Is someone else I love next?

Both Mdot and Showkey were artists, so this was no average death. It went viral. Two rapper best friends, months apart. People were reaching out to me from all over the world and my DMs were crowded with fans paying their condolences, hatemail, interviewers. It was all a bit much for me at the time and I barely responded to any of them.

One day, I got a message. The message.

This message stood out to me because it was from a woman I didn't know, showing nothing but care. It was a bit strange, I must say, but out of all my-jam packed DMs I chose to reply to this one, for some reason. To Ebinehita Iyere.

And here it begins, a new path, a new relationship. Ebi reached out with condolences and care, she explained she had her own experiences in the streets as a young girl and went on to tell me about the new path she was on.

I gave her my number and we met up.

Our first meeting was a hair appointment; she had arranged for me to get braids and I remember the hairstyle so clearly. I know it sounds absolutely bizarre to just meet up with someone from Instagram, but that just goes to show how lost and wounded I was. Our favourite spot was Nando's and, although we had only had Instagram conversations and phone calls, I felt like I had known this woman forever! She asked so many questions about me – there was some kind of urgent care she had for me. It was like being in school and having a mentor all over again, and, to be honest, at that time that's all I needed.

Ebi made promises and she never failed me. From Nando's to just being there, she always pulled through. Our relationship instantly grew with more Nando's dates and more 1-1 phone calls. I felt like God had sent a little angel on my shoulder to guide me to a better direction. I started getting into situations, pausing and remembering things Ebi had told me. She never once made rules or regulations, it was always a free space. She would never push her opinion onto me, she would only be there to guide whatever decision I made. The respect levels were mutually high and that's why I trusted her. There was no judgement, she opened up to me too, and that's why I trusted her so much.

I was still in and out of trouble, but no matter what time I called her from the police station she would answer. Ebi started to introduce me to people she worked with, and I started to see the vision; she always went on about eventually having a bigger foundation and helping more young ladies everywhere. Ebi was good to me. It felt selfish for me to keep her to myself. I introduced her to my friends who were also going through some things. She treated them the exact same: unlimited guidance and help. But we always had our thing from the start, I was her 'Shuggy' as she'd call me. Time went on and our relationship grew.

I started to understand Ebi's story more. I felt like

I was growing. In school, I'd always had a mentor, but they always left as I began to trust them. This would spark up a lot of emotions for me, as my mum did the same thing, but Ebi never left. She was always there – even the times I didn't want her there, that woman was going to show face!

Nowadays, me and Ebi may not speak for a few weeks, but the love never changes. Our relationship carved me as a woman. I had a higher calling in the mentoring lifestyle, which I wasn't aware of until Ebi came along. She made my dreams realistic, and now watching her blossom and work with other young people is even more inspiring. I am proud to be a part of Ebinehita Iyere's story and I'm sure I am not the only one.

I am now studying Counselling Level 3, going onto Level 4, and also working with a few young people as a kind of informal mentor. I hope to grow and make a bigger foundation just like Ebi has. Although I can't escape gang violence that easily, I can honestly say my life is now smoother and I am away from that mentality, with nothing but help from my angel Ebinehita Iyere.

Closing Thoughts

You've by now read *Girlhood Unfiltered*, a book letting you into but a fraction of a few of many Black girls' experiences in their childhood. What they face. What they enjoy. What they hope. Who they are and who they strive to become. These are the challenges we are facing, and this is the world Black girls are growing up in. If I could burn everything down and start again, I would want the world for Black girls to look like this: A world without injustice. A world where Black girls did not need Milk Honey Bees. Where I do not have to fight for the rights of Black girls nor the education system. I wish the world did not need this book. Yet, here we are.

We are unique. We are not one-dimensional nor linear. We are not bundled in categories or to be put into boxes with labels in the media. We do not act, look, or think alike. We are very much different and yet tied in together through our melanin and through our similarities in gender. We have different interests and different cultures. We are full of expressions and embody different personalities.

This book is another form of space for Black girls to be able to sit with the different things Black girls relate to. To accommodate your valid feelings as you read the words of others like you. With limitless potential and the invaluable values that you hold, the world does not know what they do when they tell you are not enough. You are more than enough. Even in the face of constant adultification, criminalisation of everything we do and come with, ignorance, racism, misogyny, and all these intersections, we, Black girls are everything inside and out. The pioneers of everything creative that the world judges them for.

See yourselves in truth and not how the world sees you when they look through guilty-until-proven innocent eyes. Don't judge your behaviour nor your peer's behaviour, but communicate through it. Behaviour is simply another language that is misunderstood and miscommunicated often. It is okay to not know how to express yourself, there is no rush. Take your time with everything you have read and everything you are feeling. You have time.

With the words in this book, let the honey pour into you and I wish you to hold it well. To grab every opportunity and run with it. This world is your oyster, and this life is yours to live as everything and more! And guess what? You are not alone in your journey. There are so many other young Black girls going through the same, yet different, things as you. They are also navigating their experiences in their own ways, like they just told you a few pages back. I hope this book encourages you to navigate the world in peace and not in pieces.

It is not easy to get your feet under you nor find your footing in this age of social media. Don't conform simply because somebody else is doing it; sometimes in a world of influencers, it's better to have influence and not be an influencer. However, it doesn't take from the fact that the women on the screens are phenomenal. Look up to them and remember that these women have real-life experiences as well. See the experiences that these women are showing and note that no matter where you come from, you are allowed to dream big. But, when you dream big remember where you started and remember who you are. Remember that influencers are humans first and that you can never forget to recognise humanity before their social media presence. So, love your influencers. Be proud of your influencers because they are doing things that we never could have imagined that Black women would be doing in years to come.

In the same way that the internet makes parents weary, previous organisations and projects like Milk Honey Bees were not conducted properly, or maybe had a lack of funding to be sustainable. This created reluctance in some parents in letting their child join Milk Honey bees, but I know that what lies in reluctancy is fear. There's a lack of understanding, or just a natural fear that a protector will have over a person that they are protecting, but it circles back to the relationship that we build with parents. We integrate the parent and the child into everything we do. I am beyond thankful for being able to work with parents who I have amazing relationships with and that there is an understanding that, no matter what, I place their daughter, her safety, protection, wellbeing, and education first.

In this work, I do not hold all the keys nor all the answers. My inner child is still receiving learning and education from the girls that I support, the women and girls in my family, or even on my timeline. They never fail to remind me that anything and everything is possible if they put their mind to it, but it is not just about them. It's about how the world allows them to navigate.

As much as I am a "role model" I believe I am a "real" model. I come with playing a role that I'm not necessarily playing because I'm not acting but because I take it seriously. However, I come with the realness of being human too. I have gone through experiences that should've never been experienced. I am still learning from the experience that others have been through whilst growing out of what I experienced. It is an honour to not leave the environment I had these experiences in but to instead "make it better". There are problems everywhere. It is only right to make the environment better, as when there is a problem you do not move the person, you fix the environment. This is what I believe, and this is what my work reflects.

I don't want them to have a seat at the table, but to create all their tables. I am pushing for 16 to 23-year-olds to have an extensive and an incredible CV that could never have been imagined for them to have because of their environments, but they do – rightfully so as they have always put their best foot forwards. I want to be in attendance at their many awards, their business launches, graduations, see them on billboards, be there for their learning, standing, and speaking out! I want to see our Black girls' success globally and watch them become the women of tomorrow.

I want them to put their H.E.R first. To prioritise their wellbeing, rest and appreciate their internal beauty, and to take time sitting and processing their experiences and emotions. Their feelings are valid. They are allowed to feel the way they feel. To be nurtured and cared for and praised for. Every progress is great progress.

This world is as much our world as it is everybody else's. There is space to take up even when we feel like there is none. We have words worthy of being listened to even when we are reluctant to speak. There are experiences we have the right to have. Going to school and being treated equally as every other student. Laughing out loud and being confident in our friendship groups, and not being deemed as loud and participating in antisocial behaviour. To be a girl. To be Black. To have a childhood that is not tainted by trauma. Do not wait for the world to offer you what they have when it is too late, make and take the opportunities.

Let us work on your behalf and rest. Do not grow quickly and leave your girlhood behind. It is most precious and a most fragile state to be in. Cherish your playtime and friendships and prioritise having fun by just being. By not taking on burdens. By loving life. By being you.

We are working hard, kicking the doors, and ripping them off the hinges for you to access that room you deserve to walk into. So many Black women are working today for their inner child, and for the girls of today who will be the women of tomorrow.

To became one of those women, you must heal to grow. You must play. It may not be easy, and you will know you are ready to heal when you know. The steps you take towards it only make it easier without making it easy. Do the things that you can do to nurture yourself and the things that you like even if nobody likes it, do it solo. The little ways that you support yourself makes it better along the way. You can find play within almost everything. I used to skip to the shop and that was my play. Change the colour of my gummy headphones depending on my mood was me playing with expression. Playing has many forms, it can express many emotions. Let loose your feelings even if they are negative! Play and speak to the people that you know you can confide in and find safety in. Be a bee playing and enjoying the flowers in a garden.

Some of these incredible bees could be running a Milk Honey Bees sister organisation in the future in an area they've grown up in. A Black led girl organisation is always welcome, she is welcome to ask me for help, knowledge, and tools for starting it. Milk Honey Bees exists with my mentoring skills, learned from my experiences interlinked with the advice I got along the way. It is not used to tell the girl how to live her life but to support her in her journey and every experience. In her trauma as well as in her joy. Ensuring that the sufferings of yesterday will not be the sufferings of tomorrow. Redefining Black girls' childhood and documenting it for other girls to know what their childhood should be like, as I did not have that chance to know what it should have or should not have been. Letting them live out their opportunities and giving the girls a mental tape of their experience of Black girlhood whilst documenting it on social media alongside the physical documentation of this book. It all circles back to H.E.R. I have started this organisation knowing that as much as life is a circle, it is also a straight line with so many different directions.

Life proved it to me when I realised that I'd collected my first hostel keys in the same building that I now run Milk Honey Bees from. Where I let girls come upstairs to me instead of me going downstairs and not allowing them entry, like I was denied that access before. I give them access where I was denied access. Milk Honey Bees works hard to make sure we see us affect policy changes, publish books and more.

The whole essence of Milk Honey Bees has been that Black girls matter because of their wholeness, not because of their work. Milk Honey Bees is a nest of lifetime connections and will forever be so. It is for Black girls growing up mainly, for their voice and visibility to be respected, protected and credited for everything they do in the world.

When you read this book, read it with intention of not just understanding but accepting. Do not try to find validations or lack in why we feel, or why we've done or said things in our experiences. Why we have navigated ourselves how we have. Why we did not navigate ourselves in another manner. This book is for you to listen, and to listen to us only. To not judge, but accept how young girls spent their childhood as themselves. Find your relations or lessons in the little part we have shared with you.

Girlhood Unfiltered is not just a book you hold, but genuine girlhood experiences that I have shared with you in your hands. That they have shared with the world to hold in their hands. Their firsts, the things that shouldn't have been experienced and avoided, their favourite things, how they feel, what they want to do, how the world looks at them and more. It is a book of Girlhoods that have not been censored or altered in anyway. Truly unfiltered and unapologetic. Girlhoods that I love to hear about and hurt to hear about and always give space to experience. This book is another space for them.

All I ask is that you respect it as much as they have respected giving you the opportunity to be in their space. Respect it as though when you are reading, you are in an actual conversation with them. Respect this work, this space, and the emotions it holds.

It means everything to me and more.

Ebinehita Iyere, 2022

A Letter to My 15-and-A-Half-Year-Old Self, Young Empress Who Was Seen and Not Heard

To my precious self,

You deserved so much more. You deserved your behaviour to be heard and not judged. To be catered to and understood. Behaviour is a form of communication, and your communication was loud and clear. Every experience that you experienced, the ones that have been spoken about in the book and the ones that you experienced as you grew that haven't been spoken about has shaped you, are still shaping you and will shape you to become who you are in the past, today and future all matter. We didn't think we'd be making it to 30. We also didn't think we would be doing these amazing things that I do. Living our life that we do. Let alone still having the same tenancy that you had as a teenager.

I am so proud of you for being and becoming who you wanted which is the vibrant, quirky. loud but shy, outspoken, colourful, strongly vibrant and sassy sometimes with a bit of attitude real person that you are. And everything you've endured.

I will be honest; you could've done some things differently. Thinking back to what adults said back in the day, although not communicated in the best of ways, I now do understand and see where they were coming from.

For me to even come to that conclusion, I've had to learn the art of listening, not just to support the work but to keep myself safe in life and navigate society. I've had to simply listen. I think we should've, and I wish we started listening before. We could have avoided so much if we had listened or been provided with a space to be listened to. But all in all, here we are. I am filling in the gaps and cracks where you fell through. Going from the Empress who's seen and not heard, to becoming Ebinehita, who is seen and sees others, heard and listens to others.

I am really and sincerely proud of you and how you have processed and are still processing everything. We will tell the world one day our story but right now we needed to put the girls first, so that they could put H.E.R first in these essays.

I dedicate these letters and these essays to you and the girls that grew up with us at 15 years old, to the girls in the youth clubs, those I grew up with in the hostels and to all the girls that came across the Empress and had negative or positive interactions with. This has been for you. Everything I've done to make sure that girls don't go through what we went through. This has been for our inner child. Taking a few relieving steps to healing. I am so proud of us. I am so proud of the representation that although my 15-year-old did not have it, the adult me has it and I am friends and have relationships with a lot of them. I have come undeniably far.

Yes, you still come out at times, and I love it and I will always hold on to you. You are and always will be the foundation of becoming me. To the Empress, like I always used to say. You can have so many things, but I will always be me and nobody can change that.

There are 3 parts of me. Ebi: the girl that transitioned into the Empress. If they had listened to Ebi maybe the world would not have met Empress but I am glad I met you. Everything that we went through from 15 to 22 years old happened for a reason and even though at 18 I was supposed to be an adult, the reality is I was an adult at 15 and at 18 I became 15. I have two versions of my 15-year-old self that played out at two different times. She kept me safe, and she's always kept me safe. She helped me transition into Ebinehita.

You are allowed to feel. Probably feels weird hearing that but you are. I know it still hurts at times and it's allowed. What you endured not enough pages could capture it how you processed it all is not only reflected across this book it is still an ongoing process.

Empress, I need you know that everything happens for a reason and although it wasn't the best reason, it happened! You are and always will be the best part of me because you gave me the fuel to do all this. Empress, they said so much about you never being and you became. We never thought we'd make it...

Who knew...

I owe you an apology for all the times I harmed you, hid you or allowed others to harm you. Though at times it was out of your control I'm still sorry it happened. I've learnt that looking after us was never too late and putting you first no matter the age will always be everything.

I love you and I am so proud of you.

A Letter To All The Young Black Girls, Past, Present and Future, Who, Whether They Know It Or Not, Are Milk Honey Bees Girls at Heart

I want you to see how valuable you are, so much is focused on how you externally present and not who you are and how you feel. I want you to be able to focus on yourself and what you want to achieve and navigate the world not in pieces.

To some it might sound like a pipe dream, because of the way the world is set up and systems are set up, but I want change and justice in a way that leads you to not just have a seat at the table but a whole new table that is just yours. I want you to be able to rest and play, you shouldn't have to do the work and show up for everyone all the time. I want you to travel, I want you to have to experiences, I want you to play. And to do all that without the burdens you've read about in these pages. Do what is necessary to be listened to. If you must speak louder, shout or scream, then do so. If you feel like nobody is listening, remember that we are here listening to you. Even if listening is sometimes hard, it is a necessary action to process information.

For my Milk Honey Bees, I want the same. But in the current systems you are growing up in, I want education reform and change in that system so that you can have the freedom and right to learn in a safe space without distractions, stereotypes, and judgement. I want people to learn from this book, I want them to hear your voices as they are, not as they're expected to be. I need you, reading this, to understand that the girls of today are the women of tomorrow and you shouldn't have to turn pain to power. Black girls deserve to have joy. For you, the girls, I want you to hold on to HER. You are the most important part of yourself and this journey we've been on together. You are more than your referral forms, you're more than how people see you, and what you think the world wants of you.

Know that our space is adaptable. Milk Honey Bees can be run in a park, in any physical space. Know that you are a bee and bees exist in many places and fly to many places although they are not meant to. Bees should not be able to fly, their wings and body does not match but they don't know this and continue to fly anyway. That is the same way that Black girls do not how amazing you are, yet you keep going, producing honey and sweetness for the world. Sometimes the world does not recognise us but we recognise ourselves.

Please remember to occupy space and whatever

space is. Space is wherever we create it and wherever they lead it to be. Be yourself. It's the space that you get to be yourself with no dictation.

Your Girlhood Is a work of art. Your Girlhood is UNFLITERED. You are THAT girl.

A Letter to All The Adults Who Impact Young Black Girls in Every Way

There is so much I could say and it hurts, hurts because I wish I didn't have to tell adults how to interact, respect, love and honour Black girls.

Protect Black girls. Listen to Black girls. Cherish Black girlhood.

To this very day, we see Black women leading in their industries and holding up systems without thought of whether it once held and comforted them. So with this said, Black girls are quite literally *your* future, but they shouldn't have to wait until then to even have a chance at being seen.

Let's meet them in their present. In their Black girlhood.

See her, before you speak at her.
Ask her, before you assume.
Learn how to pronounce her name.
Seek out the support she needs.

Black Girls deserve and demand a world that allows

them to be Black Girls.

Children. Not mini-women.

Unique Individuals. Not carbon copies.

Upset and angry. Not aggressive and ill-mannered.

Vulnerable. Not always strong.

Confused. Not always capable.

Healing not always healers.

Creative and credited. Not criminalised.

Dependent not just dependable.

Vocal, not voiceless.

None of this is about creating something in Black girls that wasn't there to begin with.

This is about recognising that when you live in a world that acts like it doesn't see you - you will slowly start to believe that you are invisible.

That you don't matter. When the reality you are everything and more inside and out.

Here, in black and white, is what you can do:

1. Listen to Black Girls
2. Do not ask Black Girls to shrink themselves
3. Allow Black Girls to have autonomy and live their honest truth
4. Treat Black Girls like the children they are
5. Tell Black Girls they are beautiful inside and out
6. Allow Black Girls to feel

This is about ensuring that Black Girlhood is present, not erased.

Acknowledgements

I would like to firstly thank God. I thank Him sincerely for protecting me and not leaving me in the darkest of times. For not leaving me in the happiest of moments and being there for, caring for and doing much more for me beyond my understanding. Making gold of whatever my hand has touched and protecting me from everything I have encountered. I honestly would not be here without my faith nor His guidance.

My dearest, dearest parents. My love for you is priceless and endless. I am forever bound and thankful for the life, love and light that you provided me with and continue to provide me with. I am blessed to have two parents that, although times were hard due to my behaviour and miscommunication, made sure I always knew I could be who I wanted to be. You have taught me more than anybody could teach me in your own ways. I forever am in love with being your daughter. To my sisters Ehis and Ose – I just want you to know that in everything that I do, it has meaning. The fight for Black girls includes you.

To my lovely family in Australia. You are everything to me and you all know this. You are all a home to me. My uncles and cousins who looked after 7-year-old me; I want to say thank you too. The experience at seven-years-old has now led me to having my very own fantastic Four. Chiedu, Onyeka, Onyineye and Amelia: you four changed my whole understanding of being a Black girl navigating the different spaces I took up. You inspired me to come back to the UK & to continue working with Milk Honey Bees. You really do make this fight easier as the days go by, all because I know that the fight for Black girls is global. I love you for so much, and I thank you so much for putting up with me during this writing process as well.

To my irreplaceable best friends Rita, Judy, Vanessa, Folu and Chantel. Essentially thank you for the support, the memories and for ensuring I got this done. Kaiden, my Godson, I want to let you know that you changed my life. You came at a time where I could have simply given up. Just you being you kept me going. I thank you for the hugs, kisses, and the love. Thank you for reminding me that I have indeed come a long way. I am so proud of everything. I value everything dearly and it all stems from you.

To the teachers who neglected me and who gave up on me... I have nothing but this book and these girls to evidence that NO Black Girl will amount to nothing. The teachers that believed in me, I just want to thank you.

Winston. There is so much to say, but no words measure up to the thank you's I'd like to give you. I don't think you will ever understand what you did for me when you did it. I guess through annoyance and grief, you supported me to create a platform that has now gone on to do what it is doing. I will forever be thankful to you, Whitney Illes and Jenni Steele for allowing me to grow, work, support and be supported by Juvenis. You are appreciated. You are loved. You are an impactful piece that can be never be removed from me. You are truly credited for everything you have done and do.

All the professionals, organisations and partners that supported Milk Honey Bees. We thank you for your time, your patience, your learnings, your resources, and your dedication. Thank you for always amplifying the voices of Milk Honey Bees and Black girls even beyond Milk Honey Bees. It is truly notable work you do with us, and it is truly notable work you support us with.

Gyamfia Osei, I thank you from the bottom of my heart for being a support. Knights Of: Aimée, Tia, Ella, Annabelle. Tia and Karis for the stunning cover. Thank you all for taking the risk to create something so beautiful with and for us. I hope this opens another door in the publishing world. I hope it also inspires many other young people to know that they can write and get into publishing. Doors are always meant to be opened and never to stay closed. Thank you for believing in our work and inspiring the readers who will open our book.

Of course, our editor Eishar, who absolutely has been with us through every step of the journey. Might have also accidentally become a youth worker at times because she was doing sessions with the girls. I thank you for the empathy, the love, the care that you showed the girls and me. For understanding and taking time to understand too. Thank you for sitting down and listening.

The girls who I supported when I did not know I was supporting them; please never think that I have forgotten you. That will never be possible. Never in a million years. Do not ever feel like the existence of Milk Honey Bees has erased your experience with me. Milk Honey Bees is here now, and you are too. I will forever hold onto what we had and how we grew. I see you all, I remember you all and I am truly immensely so proud of you all.

To all the girls that are supported through Milk Honey Bees: you must know that you are and always will be my why. I cannot thank you enough for allowing me to work with and for you. I thank you for the tears, the laughs, the headaches, the stealing of my charger, the not turning up on time. I thank you for the frustration. The pride I feel. The emotional rollercoaster we all ride together. I thank you for being all in for me as I am all in for you. I thank you for it all. I am truly grateful for having the privilege of experiencing each and every single one of you.

To the 20 girls that wrote and contributed to this book: I thank you massively. I thank you and I want you to know how proud we all are. How proud of yourselves you should be. A majority of you wrote during your GCSEs, a time of being under stress and under pressure. All of you wrote during the most crucial times of your adolescence. I want you to know that you made it. You did that. This book has been created for you and by you, and without you none of it would be possible. These words will travel and touch people that are like you, will be like you and have been like you. You can only imagine my emotions when I think of Milk Honey Bees and the work we do. This book will forever carry a piece of it. Be as proud as I am of you and be proud of the words this book holds.

About the Author

Ebinehita Iyere is founder of Milk Honey Bees – a project that allows young Black women and girls to put H.E.R first while exploring their creativity and gaining skills to navigate society. She is a Therapeutic Youth Practitioner who supports the emotional needs of young people in the community, especially those affected by the education and youth justice system. Ebinehita also works with professionals and decision makers to ensure the voices of young people are reflected across policies that affect them.

About Knights Of

Knights Of is a multi-award-winning inclusive publisher focused on bringing underrepresented voices to the forefront of commercial children's publishing. With a team led by women of colour, and an unwavering focus on their intended readership for each book, Knights Of works to engage with gatekeepers across the industry, including booksellers, teachers and librarians, and supports non-traditional community spaces with events, outreach, marketing and partnerships.

If you or someone you know has been affected by any of the issues mentioned in this book, here are some places you can turn to for support:

Milk Honey Bees: www.milkhoneybees.co.uk
Juvenis: www.juvenis.org.uk
Project Yana: www.jennisteele.co.uk/yana-project
The Black, African and Asian Therapy Network: www.baatn.org.uk

Bayo; a space to find support services run by and for the Black community: bayo.ubele.org

Bullying
Anti-Bullying Alliance: www.anti-bullyingalliance. org.uk
Childline: 0800 11 11 (24/7 helpline)
The Mix: www.themix.org.uk

Self-harm, depression, and other mental health challenges
Mind: www.mind.org.uk
HOPELINEUK: 0800 068 4141
Text YM to YoungMind's Textline on 85258
The Mix: www.themix.org.uk
Alumina: www.selfharm.co.uk

Death of a parent or loved one
Hope Again: www.hopeagain.org.uk
Winston's Wish: 08088 020 021

Gang-related violence
The Mix: www.themix.org.uk
Juvenis: www.juvenis.org.uk

Emotional abuse and abusive relationships
Kidscape: www.kidscape.org.uk
Respect Not Fear: www.respectnotfear.co.uk
Southall Black Sisters: www.southallblacksisters.
org.uk

Project Yana: www.jennisteele.co.uk/yana-project

Entering care or leaving the care system
Coram Voice: www.coramvoice.org.uk
National Youth Advocacy Service: www.nyas.net
Catch 22: www.catch-22.org.uk
Sister System: www.sistersystem.org

Support for LGBTQ+ teenagers
Mermaids: www.mermaidsuk.org.uk
Stonewall: www.stonewall.org.uk